The Individual, the Enterprise and the State

The Individual, the Enterprise and the State

A collection of ideas and insights from a series of seminars held at the Oxford Centre for Management Studies, England.

Edited by R. I. Tricker (Director of the Centre)

With contributions from:

Lord Armstrong
Sir Ian Bancroft
Henry Boettinger
David Harris
Jacques G. Maisonrouge
Sir Bernard Miller
Lord Ryder
Dick Taverne
Graham Turner
Bill Weinstein

A HALSTED PRESS BOOK

JOHN WILEY & SONS
New York – Toronto

*English language edition, except U.S.A. and Canada
published by*
Associated Business Programmes Ltd
17 Buckingham Gate, London SW1

Published in USA and Canada by
Halsted Press, a Division of John Wiley & Sons Inc
New York

First published 1977

Library of Congress Catalogue Card No: 77 – 78350

ISBN 0–470–99211–5

© Robert I. Tricker, Oxford 1977

Typeset by Computacomp (UK) Ltd., and
printed in Great Britain by
A. Wheaton & Co., Exeter

Contents

Introduction

The idea of power has fascinated man's imagination over the centuries. The ability to make things happen, as Mary Parker Follet (1) once defined power, is fundamental to the achievement of personal ambition, corporate objectives or social aims. It is also central to the practice of management. Surprisingly managers and writers about management have only turned their attention to the notion of power quite recently; although it features in many discussions now between executives. From management at shop floor level to the taking of strategic decisions about the long term future of the firm, managers feel that their rights and authority have been eroded.

For generations managers have acted confidently in the belief that promotion into the appropriate box on the organisation chart conferred power. Loyalty, respect and recognition of authority came with the key to the executive wash room, the named car parking space and the seat in the senior diningroom. Discussing their management style, such executives tend to perceive themselves as friendly, supportive, benign — able to create a climate in which the team want to achieve, with them, the corporate goals. 'With communication and participation, delegation of responsibility with proper accountability, I achieve results.' But what if commitment is not achieved? What if others insist on pursuing different goals?

At the strategic decision making level, too, there is a feeling that the old freedom to take decisions has been lost.

'Instead of setting tough-minded goals and driving hard to achieve them for the benefit of everyone concerned, I find myself seeking consensus in a welter of competing interest groups.' The traditional roles of the business corporation are also being questioned. The interests of groups outside the classical firm have to be recognised. Demands for accountability and access to information challenge the legitimacy of the enterprise in society today. Increasingly the state seems to be involved in areas previously the exclusive realm of corporate affairs.

Thus middle managers report a feeling of being less able to make things happen, more of operating in a vacuum; and senior executives complain that some of their entrepreneurial freedoms are being lost. Where has the power moved? On what basis does the power of modern management lie? Is the apparent shift towards large and impersonal organisations and the corporate state, with a diminuation of the significance of the individual, really occuring? What *is* the legitimate role of business in society today?

Executives meeting in the Oxford Management Centre recently have been exploring such issues. Two years ago political aspects of the manager's job were introduced into the study of management, looking at the changing social, economic and political environment facing the management decision-maker. The interest thus kindled led me to suggest the series of seminars on the individual, the enterprise and the state which form the basis of this book.

The study of the political context of management has provided a new dimension for many managers. It contrasts dramatically with the emphasis of teaching in the Centre for its first ten years. Then the focus was on numeracy, computers, models and management science, behavioural theories and management techniques. Not that such areas have become less important, but the additional focus today emphasises the growing complexity and interrelatedness of management. Increasingly, as well as involving analysis and measurement, management has a political component, which for some managers is new. Confident in attitudes and values inherited from previous generations only now do they recognise that many of the principles underlying their managerial practice are, themselves, based on ideologies which relate the individual and the enterprise to society. Ideas about the nature of work, the ethics of growth, democracy, human rights, including the right of ownership and privileges and power, are not fundamental truths but beliefs. Much that has been taken for granted as basic and 'the way things are' is open to discussion and revision.

Such explorations can be stimulating and provocative, particularly if they seem to be directly related to the changing situation that managers face. Of course these issues are not new. As Paul Tillich (2) points out in his seminal work on the individual 'from Plato and Aristotle, the concept of power plays an important role in ontological thought.' Subsequently Locke & Paine, Rousseau & Burke, Kafka & Sartre were each, in their way, battling with the issues of individualisation versus participation, people as individuals and as part of a state. Consequently the concerns now facing managers have ancient roots. When pursued they extend far beyond the bounds of managers' ability to make things happen to root questions about the role, values and relationships of individuals, enterprises and states.

In medieval times the master had very considerable powers over his serf, just as an owner did over his slaves until quite recently. During the Middle Ages a king exercised power over his subjects, chopping off their heads or throwing them into the dungeons as necessary. Although the idea of individual freedom was well established in England by the fourteenth century, much earlier than in Continental Europe incidentally, the Lord of the Manor — the land lord — exercised considerable power through his ownership of land. Though the ownership changed over the centuries, the power vested in land survived through to the eighteenth century or later. In the nineteenth century, with the industrial revolution in mining and manufacturing bringing movement to the towns and new employment, considerable power shifted to the employer able to offer employment and threaten its loss. The twentieth century was swaddled in this cloak at its birth; it is the mantle of authority still worn by some managers today.

But what sanctions are now available? Much has been curtailed by the state. At the same time is the manager's ability to cause change being diffused towards smaller groups able and prepared to take action — consumer groups making demands on manufacturers, the workers who seize their factory to prevent its sale, bread van delivery drivers refusing supplies to maintain resale prices, computer operators, toolroom workers, power engineers ... all able by their position to take action? Examples are legion of this shift in power in Western society.

The opportunity to think about some of these issues was provided in the seminars mounted during the winter of 1976. Ten distinguished contributors, drawn from business, political life, the civil service and academic backgrounds were invited to address themselves to the broad theme *the individual, the enterprise and the state*. Their presentations have now been collected together, and give a wide sweep of viewpoints and interests.

A heartening confidence in the individual's ability to stand out against unacceptable excesses of state control is expressed by Lord Armstrong. Apparent trends to collectivist, more centralised types of society could be exaggerated, he suggests; individuals in Britain were showing their ability 'to get out from under'. Another claim for the primacy of the individual comes from Jacques Maisonrouge — Chairman and Chief Executive of IBM Europe, a company that has fostered the idea of individual opportunity within a paternalistic framework. The modern multinational, he argues, is a necessary bastion against state domination. Graham Turner, on the other hand, expresses his fears of an unrecognised slide towards the corporate state, quoting examples from supposedly free countries in which people feel constrained to think the thoughts known to be acceptable to the group.

Dick Taverne, in a spirited defence of liberal traditions, also focuses on the individual, spelling out the implications of less state involvement in the lives of people and the need for a new alignment in party political terms in Britain. Looking at the enterprise, both Sir Bernard Miller and David Harris offer alternative forms of corporate organisation. An end to equity shareholding, is Harris's approach, as an alternative to the essentially mid-nineteenth century idea of corporations owned, manipulated and controlled by shareholders or their nominees. Sir Bernard draws on his long experience as Chairman of the John Lewis Partnership to recommend employee partnership.

Relationships between enterprise and state are considered by both Sir Ian Bancroft and Lord Ryder, the latter developing his hopes for the National Enterprise Board to bridge the gap between state and enterprise. Behind each of the three sides of the triangle in the title — individual to state, state to enterprise and enterprise to individial — there are basic, philosophical issues. Henry Boettinger and Bill Weinstein pursue some of them. Though essentially the balance between power, will and freedom is fundamental in every civilisation, the particular balance between state co-ordination and personal liberties, between social welfare of the community and opportunities for private success, have to be pursued anew in today's situation.

As managerial sanctions inherited from the nineteenth century disappear and other sectors of society show that they are prepared to use the sanctions that lie in their hands,

new forms of management and new approaches to
corporate decision making have to be imagined. Thus new
relationships between individual, enterprise and state have
to be evolved. It is as difficult as ever to find a utopia in
which stability of the state, economic growth and
opportunity are kept consistent with individual liberty.

These seminar papers are published in the hope that by
stimulating further discussion they might contribute to the
evolution of ideas. I am very grateful to each of the
contributors for allowing their paper to be published, often
after considerable pains in polishing their own scripts, and
sometimes after submitting to inexorable editing by me.

Writing many decades ago R.H. Tawney (3) suggested that
'it is obvious that no change of system or machinery can
avert those causes of social malaise which exist in egotism,
greed or quarrelsomeness of human nature. What it can do
is create an environment in which those are not the
qualities which are encouraged. It cannot secure that men
live up to their principles. It can establish their social order
upon principles which, if they please, they can live up to and
not live down. It cannot control their actions. It can offer
them an end on which to fix their minds. And, as their
minds are, so in the long run and with exceptions their
practical activity will be'.

Not since those brief, exciting days of the British
Republic, following the execution of Charles I by the
soldiers of the Long Parliament in the seventeenth century
has there been as much questioning of values, roles and
relationships of state and individuals. And those were the
days when the protestant ethic was formulated — individual
freedom, parliamentary sovereignty, and the right to
ownership of property and pursuit of profit. Today's
discussions could lead the future historian to record the tail-
end of the twentieth century as the watershed of Western
ideology or a threshold step to something greater.

References

1 Mary Parker Follet in Metcalf & Urwick, *Dynamic Administration — the collected papers of Mary Parker Follet*, Pitman, 1941.

2 Paul Tillich, *The Courage to be*, Nisbet & Co., 1952, Fontana, 1962.

3 R.H. Tawney, *The Acquisitive Society*, Penguin, 1938.

1 Some aspects of politics and power in our time

Henry Boettinger

Henry Boettinger is Director of Corporate Planning AT&T New York. An engineer from John Hopkins University with graduate work in Michigan and New York University Graduate School, he has spent his career largely within the Bell System including operating appointments with the Chesapeake and Potomac Telephone Company and financial appointments with AT&T New York. He has also been Vice President and Comptroller of the Michigan Bell Telephone Company and Director of Management Sciences before being appointed Director of Corporate Planning in 1972.

He is a Visiting Fellow of the Oxford Centre for Management Studies and an Adjunct Professor of Pace University. His publications include 'Moving Mountains, Or The Art and Craft of Letting Others see Things Your Way,' Macmillan 1969 as well as essays in various published collections.

Excursions to political philosophy encounter obstacles and traps inherent in any subject which attempts to *describe* and *prescribe* simultaneously. In addition, politics deals with 'conflict-defining' and 'conflict-resolving' human activity, and thus its discussions must forego the settled calm and empiricism of scientific discourse. Everyone engaged is an advocate or critic of the subject matter and its interpretations.

In this context, it may be useful to distinguish the three classes of 'knowledge' available to us. These are

Facts

Analytical inferences

Value judgments

The acquisition and assembly of facts require the apparatus and discipline of scholarship to settle disputes. Analytical inferences, drawn from facts, are the province of theory or thought-systems and use the disciplines of logic, mathematics, statistics, and hypothesis-testing. But value judgments are rooted in taste, mood, experience, prejudice, and preferences — all of which can be non-rational, emotional or genetically influenced. The only methods available to settle value questions are politics and force. We should not be surprised that value judgments dominate other forms of knowledge in political discussions, and this paper is no exception. However, perhaps an attempt to give a new angle of view may help illuminate some of the troublesome aspects that attend present relations among the individual, the enterprise, and the state.

New wine in old bottles

Two seminal thinkers of our civilization, Plato and Aristotle, lived in troubled times which triggered their speculative talents to address the merits of different forms of government. They discerned four basic types, and saw them as changing from one to another as the abuses inherent in their extreme forms would call forth a new phase, either by violent or peaceful means. The forms are equally applicable to any organization, from a family to a large corporation, when considering the forms of its 'governance'.

The cycle of forms looks like this:

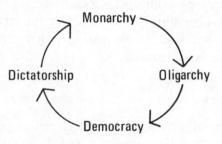

Monarchy was seen as the 'most natural' form, since it seemed the most stable and legitimate, but as the monarch needed expert helpers, skilled in different fields to meet developing complexities, an aristocracy would form, from whom a few leaders (oligarchy) would take over more and more functions, though nominally 'in the name of' the monarch. (Modern bureaucracies are oligarchic.) As the oligarchy increased and abused its power over citizens, calls for democratic control by nascent leaders would result in 'the people' taking over rule of themselves. After an initial euphoria, breakdowns, inefficiencies and conflicts would result in disenchantment and the call for a strong man to rescue the community from chaos. Thus dictatorship grows in fields manured by disappointment and the cacaphony of feckless assemblies. In fact, an historian of our era, writing a century from now would see the first half of the twentieth century as a period when democracy was transformed into dictatorship in many of the world's nations. Yet, the dictator suffers from both a lack of legitimacy and problems of succession. These cause him to strive for the trappings —

and reality — of monarchy. Jumped-up, mercenary captains of Italian cities patronizing artists, and Napoleon marrying a royal princess are old examples (though setting up impressive palaces and residences are more common to contemporary dictators). Thus, the Greeks saw government in a constant cycle with various states existing contemporaneously under the different phases. We can see the same ourselves. Mankind is a contentious species and all his institutions constantly evolve under the stress of success and failure, the clash of aspirations with reality, and the tensions of flesh and spirit.

Political theory

In the history of political thought, certain 'great books' symbolise and crystallise the *Zeitgeist* of their authors. But we remember only those that celebrate regimes which survived, and, as Parkinson has observed, the books are usually written *after* the events or systems are established. Consider this short list of thinkers and activists whose ideas have shaped — and still shape — our own ideas of government:

Plato	Bacon	Rousseau
Aristotle	Hobbes	Madison
Dante	Locke	Mill
Machiavelli	Halifax	Marx
More	Bentham	Mao

Like geological strata, we erect our own programmes for progress on their heritage, but none has addressed *our* specific political problems, unique to our time, though they furnish the foundation of discourse. We are unlikely to find programatic guides from them, of value for today. Why not?

I believe that, in the last few decades, the instability of politics is rooted in the change in the number of 'players', i.e., it has changed from a 'two-person game' to a 'three-person game'. Let me explain.

Nearly all the writers above addressed the relations between the individual and the state as the primary focus of politics:

State $\rightleftharpoons$ Individual

Some gave more weight to the welfare of the individual, others more to the welfare of the state, but two-element relations are more stable than three, which suffer, both in theory and practice, inherent instabilities as the combinations of power, influence, alliances and disaffection, cause shifts in dominance. If one adds the element of *institutions* to the older ones of state and individual, we get *six* relationships instead of two:

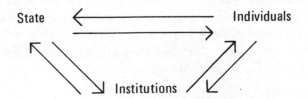

Institutions, like business, labour unions, churches, military and civil services, international bodies, education and health services, are all political forces. There is no comprehensive dynamic theory — or perhaps can never be — to explain and predict their behaviour under stress. Add to this the *complexity of discourse* which ensues when a programme or policy must traverse the obstacles of self-interest and misunderstanding when one or the other elements of individuals, enterprise, and the state undertake to mobilize support:

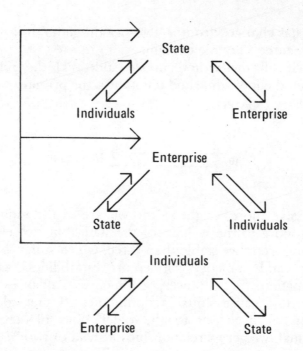

All communications take place along one or more of the paths (marked with arrows) and reactions reverberate and resonate in the mass media. It is remarkable when *any* programme today achieves a long enough run of mobilised assent to become a reality.

The polarities of preference

Since politics does deal with controversy about both means and ends, its framework of concepts consists of antithetical ideas. Yet each of these ideas is important and a case can be made for embracing it as the central focus of action in a particular set of circumstances. In fact, one can use these next three sets of lists to produce a political speech on any subject whatever, extolling those ideas congruent with your own programme, and characterising your opponent's programme as an embodiment of the antagonistic labels.

Set I

COMPETITION *vs.* COOPERATION

Rivalry	Planning
Innovation	Stability
Results	Process
Ends	Means
Power	Equity

Since political combat is carried out by human beings, the specific dramas played out will be determined by those infinite variations of motivators and restraints of the human species which we call temperament. For convenience, we can see the seven capital sins as basic motivators and the seven cardinal virtues (four from Plato, three from St. Paul) as the prime restraints. (An analogy can be found in how the muscles and instincts of a naturally spirited horse can be carried to heights of performance only by the training, bridle, reins, and heels of an intelligent master.)

Set II

CAPITAL SINS ⇄ CARDINAL VIRTUES

Pride	Courage
Anger	Justice
Gluttony	Prudence
Envy	Temperance
Sloth	Faith
Lust	Hope
Avarice	Charity

As human beings assemble in groups, institutions, or even nations, such aggregations take on the attributes of both sins and virtues, at least in the eyes of their critics and adherents.

To focus on our own era, I believe the crucial issue to be that between democracy (in its enlightened sense) and technocracy. The complexities of our highly-strung, technologically-based societies make a drift toward technique nearly irresistible. But the will to individual freedom and self-worth must constantly exercise selective and wise restraint against a mindless acceptance which would lead to a spiritless alienation — the very negation of what a good society should be.

Consider this last list in the light of the various problems and alternative solutions now under discussion as advocates hurl their labels back and forth:

Set III

DEMOCRACY *vs.* TECHNOCRACY

Freedom	Tyranny
'Athens'	'Sparta'
Humanity	Efficiency
Stagnation	'Progress'
'Weakness'	'Strength'
Diversity	Uniformity
Ferment	Stability
Empirical	Scientific
Egalitarian	Elite
Randomness	Rigidity

The most we can hope for in such contention is a pulsating equilibrium, where extremes are at least avoided, and complementarity prevails. This follows from the essential paradox of man, the ultimate building block of all human systems, however complex. Two conflicting desires exist simultaneously in every person:

1   The desire to identify with something *larger* than himself (group, nation, etc.)
2   The desire to be *unique*, to stand out as something different and apart.

We see this in the twin compulsions toward immersion and isolation, involvement and withdrawal. Again the Greeks knew the phenomenon and coined names for the two states: *agape*, for love of others and community; *eros*, for love of self and inward gratification. The words may be old, but the ideas are as relevant as tommorow.

Some aspects of a society

No fable is more applicable to an approach to the grand strategies of politics than that of the blind men and the elephant. Each inferred something different about the nature of an elephant from the limited evidence gathered by his hands feeling a section of the beast different from that of his colleagues. So too in taking a perspective toward a specific society. Consider just these six aspects:

Economic	Political
Technological	Artistic
Social	Religious

It may help to see a society as a cube in space, which presents different faces to us as we move around it or as it revolves in three dimensions. (The revolving process is similar to that where different *types* of problems emerge from time to time. Some aspects decline in importance as others rise to dominate our attention, often to the point of preoccupation.)

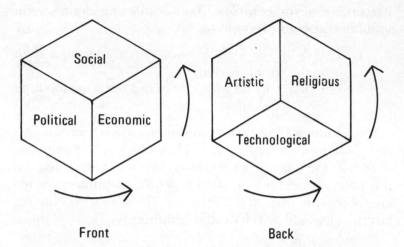

When we attempt to construct or reform any human or physical system which has several aspects, we enter the realm of *design*, a domain where art prevails over science. Politics itself has been characterized as 'the art of the possible', and the implications of constraints in the phrase are similar to the constraints which affect all artistic endeavour. Analysis is the method of science; synthesis the method of art. Utopias, constitutions, laws, and programmes are syntheses, not analyses, though examination of possible consequences should inform their creative thrust.

Sensible approaches to the design of a society require decisions — or, at least, agreement — on the following items which are present in any design:

Aim
Selection
Rejection
Arrangement
Relations between elements
Constraints
Criteria of effectiveness

One searches almost in vain for examples of current political proposals which meet these essential elements of good design, either implicitly or explicitly. We should not, therefore, be surprised that so many well-intentioned efforts so often fail.

In all designs there is some form of 'glue' which holds their parts together — and politics is no exception. In all political systems that glue is *power*.

Some reflections on power

Bertrand Russell in his brilliant, thin book on this most difficult concept (labelled simply, *Power*) distinguished three forms of power in human affairs:

1 Direct physical power over a person's body
2 Ability to grant rewards and inflict punishment
3 Influence on opinion.

He illustrated, with animal metaphors, the ways one can get a person to move in a direction preferred by one who possesses power:

1 A pig can best be placed in a van by physically lifting it in a sling (force).
2 A donkey is moved best by use of carrots or sticks (reward and punishment).
3 A horse is maneuvered by subjecting it to previous training and then using stimuli and reflexes geared to that training (education of opinion).
4 A flock of sheep are turned by influencing their leader and the rest quickly follow (influence through imitation).

Thus any leader or follower in politics is engaged in a power relationship and will use and experience all of the above forms as the relationship continues. Yet power, though essential, is not sufficient to produce the 'good society'. John Stuart Mill's two criteria for assessing good government suggest that something more is needed. His tests for judging a government were:

1 By the degree in which it tends to increase the good qualities in the governed.
2 By the efficiency with which it harnesses these qualities for public needs.

With a slight shift from efficiency to *effectiveness*, I submit the following relationship as a guide to seeing the interplay of power and individual qualities in any polity, from individuals in a family, business, government department on up to a nation:

$$Power \times Authority = Effectiveness$$

The relationship is *multiplicative*, not additive, and every person's power is always greater than zero.

The attributes of power and authority I define in the following way:

Power	x	Authority = Effectiveness
is		is
↓		↓
Conferred		Earned
Collective		Personal
Position-related		Knowledge-related
Described by formal organisation		Described by network of informal organisations

Power, in a specific case or position, is inherently limited, but personal authority is completely open-ended — and can be increased or decreased by a person's growth or decline. It is also altered — for better or worse — by an individual's response to specific events and situations. Here are a few examples of the phenomenon:

1 A recent president of the US, whose power was perhaps the greatest of anyone in the world, continually declined in authority under pressure of scandal. His power remained constant, but his effectiveness plummeted to a point requiring resignation.

2 A first-class expert in some job is promoted to a higher position in a field new to him. His effectiveness may drop, even with increased power, because he has diminished in personal authority. When his effectiveness drops to the point of incompetence, we see the foundation for the Peter Principle.

3 A manager of average performance is placed under a superior who takes the trouble to teach him the art of management, by example and training. As the manager's authority increases, his effectiveness grows, though formal power remains constant. This is the entire justification for management development programmes, and, in fact, all education. To assume, as many do, that mere serving of time in a position will increase personal authority sets up the conditions of comedy and tragedy. This is especially prevalent in politics and their supporting bureaucracies, though every institution suffers its burden of burnt-out cases. There is a vast difference between twenty years' experience and one year's experience repeated twenty times.

If one accepts this view of the relation between power, authority, and effectiveness, the futility of some current approaches to 'solving' political and social problems becomes apparent. The overall effectiveness of any group of persons engaged in a joint, purposeful activity can only occur by increasing the personal authority of the individuals who make up the group.

In this connection consider one pervasive phenomenon of our time: the tendency for an excessive flow of decisions to the topmost layers of government, business and other institutions. I believe this is due to one or more of the following weaknesses:

1   Lack of clear policy
     ('Just what are we trying to do?')
2   Ambiguous performance criteria
     ('Damned if you do, damned if you don't.')
3   Malfunction or poor organization design
     ('Whose pigeon is this? It's certainly not mine.')
4   Attempt to substitute power for authority
     ('This is bigger than both of us. Only the people upstairs can safely decide.')

In my opinion, the last is now a bit out of hand. In foreign affairs, only a Foreign Secretary is worth talking to, and excessive faith in summit meetings leads to disappointed expectations and cynicism.

Thus, the central, long-run task of politics today is to increase the personal authority of the individual *in* politics. When Plato was an old man, he addressed in *The Laws* that some problem of governance which inspired *The Republic* of his youth. After all those intervening years of observation and events, he came to the conclusion that a good government was one where good people were given *personal* responsibility subject to *popular* control. It is probably still the best we can do, but it is *our* task to define for our time what is meant by a 'good' person and which constituencies (e.g., owners, employees, capital, unions, consumers, etc.) will exercise the popular control, and how they will do it.

2 A personal view

Lord Armstrong

In introducing Lord Armstrong at the seminar Mr. Clifford Barclay (Chairman of the Oxford Management Centre's Council) said: 'Lord Armstrong has achieved a record of two classical honours in Oxford — a first in Mods. in 1936 and in Greats in 1938, the year in which he entered the Civil Service. In 1943 he became Private Secretary to the Secretary of the War Cabinet; in 1946 moved over to the Treasury; in 1962 became joint Permanent Secretary to the Treasury; in 1968 Head of the Civil Service and in 1974 decided, after thirty-six years in the Civil Service, to retire and become a Director and subsequently Chairman of the Midland Bank. He is also a Director of Shell. May I say that a record such as that covers the whole spectrum of the world in which we are involved:— the individual, the enterprise and the state. I know him best as William Armstrong the individual, the world knows him extremely well as Sir William Armstrong the servant of the state and he is now, as Lord Armstrong, head of a great enterprise.'

Introduction

May I say first of all that I am treating this literally as a
seminar. I am not going to give a lecture — I couldn't
anyway and certainly not in Oxford. Oxford still intimidates
me; so the last thing I can do is stand up and deliver a
lecture. What I am going to do is talk about the individual,
the enterprise and the state, particularly about the
relationships between them and the way I think they are
developing. I would ask you to keep in mind throughout,
even though some things I say appear to contradict it, that
in my view, of the three things that I am asked to talk about
— the individual, the enterprise and the state — only the
first is real, the individual. There are people in this
University who would argue about that reality, but let us for
the moment assume that we can agree that we are all here,
not just each one of us in his own private world, that we are
a group of individuals and that we are real. It is in that sense
that there is no reality in the word 'enterprise' or the word
'state'. Each of them signifies in effect a set of rules by which
a group of individuals behaves. At the end of the day there
are no enterprises, no states — only people. The only reality
we have to talk about are people in their various
relationships with each other, which of course can vary and
be highly important through their places in the network of
individual relationships that makes up what we call an
enterprise or a state.

The individual and the state

Take first of all the relationship between the individual and
the state: in other words between the individual in his
individual capacity and the collection of other individuals
and people who have a place in the state — I think that the
first and most obvious point is the overwhelming feeling

that many people have in Britain, and very likely in other places too, that the state has been inexorably growing in power and pervasiveness and that it is getting very near to smothering the individual. There is of course a great deal of sheer experience of that, far more than I want to deny; but I want also slightly to question it. There seems to me to be a tremendous lot of life left in the individual yet.

What seems to me interesting is not so much the way the state is encroaching on what used to be thought of as the freedoms of the individual so much as the ways in which the individual is getting out from under.

Now it is perfectly obvious that the people in this country think their taxes are too high. I say that not because of any voting results or public opinion polls but because I have not met anybody who is not trying to dodge them and that goes from the top to the bottom, right the way through from the people who occupy themselves and their tax advisers in schemes for minimising the amount of tax they pay, right down to the chap who says 'if you pay me in pound notes I will do it for two-thirds of the price'. It seems to me that this demonstrates that people think their taxes are too high. They are not quite ready to say that therefore government expenditure is too high, because the connection between taxation and expenditure has got a bit blurred, but they certainly think the taxes are too high and are busy finding ways of getting out from under. You can multiply the variety of ways in which individuals keep finding ways round the impositions, regulations and controls of the state. I suspect almost all of us have had some building alteration or addition carried out which is illegal, for which we did not get proper permission. This is virtually certain. Anybody who owns any property at all will have done something to it quite innocently for which he should have got permission. I quite agree that when you come to the big job it is another matter; but on the whole you can pay reasonable attention to the big job — it is all this little nonsense that is so trying.

It seems that means are being discovered and that the individual is beginning to assert himself. You may say these are very small signs but I want to come to some others.

Most states, if not all, came into being and then remained in being through war, through the apparent necessity to defend themselves against their neighbours or the desire to attack them. Families or tribes became kingdoms and states through settling a piece of territory and defending it, trying to extend it and so on. There is little doubt that the oldest piece of apparatus of the state is the army. In recent times the rise of nation states has been associated with wars and the necessity, as each of them saw it, to maintain armies and defences to maintain their position against others.

Now one of the phenomena of the last few years is that, leaving out the super powers, the necessity for maintaining this attitude is getting less and less important. It is a fact that we are further from total war — the war involving the whole nation — now than we have been at any time this century and we are going further and further away from it. As this happens the weapons of politicians suddenly appear to be blunt; they no longer have the alibis. Think of the situation between the two World Wars. Emerging out of World War I, we get into frightful economic crises, social crises and depression — how do we get out of it? By the emergence of the threat of another war. We are able to push aside and forget about all the social problems which are piling up because the enemy is at the gate. The good old cry goes round again, the trumpet is sounded and everybody springs to attention. But today that is not the case. Politicians lament. What do they lament? They lament the lack of the Dunkirk spirit, for heaven's sake, as if they would like there to be another Dunkirk so as to keep up hope and spirit. The weapons of politicians, the traditional attitudes of statesmen to the people were forged, framed and built in times of war, or rumours of war. When that disappears they are left faintly helpless. Here is another area where the state, as it has been known in Western Europe for many years, is becoming dubious and losing some of its self-confidence. Of course, none of this is new; the search for a substitute for war is a slogan that has been around for some time. Some people think they can find it in international economic competition. Or failing that, there is always the World Cup or Wimbledon or the Olympics.

Another change in attitude of mind that I detect is the number of people who do not really care what country they live in. There are signs of people willing to take the whole world as their oyster and think about the possibility of living in a variety of different places. There is not the same attachment to the particular bit of the planet they happen to find themselves born in.

Two other things are happening: the territorial integrity of states is no longer quite as obvious as it was. When I was young the thought that the United Kingdom would ever be anything other than the United Kingdom was unthinkable. It was the United Kingdom and there it was. Now the possibility of an independent Scotland is openly discussed and is, in my mind, more probable than not. That will carry Wales with it, Ulster will have to be tipped over the edge and there you are with four and even conceivably five members of the UN. No trouble — most of them will be well up the list in terms of numbers of population so that there is nothing stupid about it. Except it is not the way we were brought up. So territorial integrity is beginning to become questioned. I do not have to mention Quebec in Canada; you can think of other examples. I doubt if Yugoslavia will stay the way it is to the end of the century. There are the two Germanys, what is going to happen to them? So here again the state, as we know it, is quietly dissolving before our eyes. I do not mean anything dramatic, it may take a hundred years or so. I think a dissolving process is beginning. Then Britain has joined the European Community. We are passing more law-making across to a collection, a grouping of states. It is dissolving from the top as well. I might have thrown in on the way, the UN. The UN states are to be thought of not only in relation to citizens but in relationship to each other. The UN is the stage on which they all dance and to be a member of the UN is being recognised as a state. A group succeeded in calling themselves Biafra a little while ago so that made them a state. Another lot coined the word Bangladesh and low and behold they became a state. Both the coming into existence and the crumbling of states is going on before our very eyes. If you take Africa as a whole nobody can draw lines that would be on that map by the end of the century. I am not talking about whites vs. blacks, I mean blacks vs. blacks, as they get back to the natural boundaries that the colonial empires ignored, sort themselves into their tribes, federations and hunting grounds, capture the mines and other natural resources and so on. I think there is going to be a turmoil there of states coming into existence and being suppressed again for the next hundred years or more.

So the main point I want to make about the state in its relationship to the individual, is that the individual is real and alive and has his own secret ways of getting out from under whatever happens to him; whereas the state, I think, is showing a fair amount of decay.

The individual and the enterprise

Now I want to come to the enterprise, sitting somewhere in the middle, you might say, between the state on the one hand, and the individual on the other. The first thing I want to say about an enterprise is that most of them are different from either individuals or states in that they have a single goal or at least a set of readily identifiable purposes or objectives. I know individuals have purposes but for individuals these are often short lived, small and self-contradictory. Of course it is theoretically possible to give yourself a purpose and live your whole life to accomplish that purpose. It is not easy to define a purpose which is really feasible from this point of view because of the inconvenient fact of death coming at the end.

But you could actually take on and spend the whole of your life trying to succeed: but very few people do that. I do not think the state can be said to have a purpose or an objective. Anybody who wants to give it one is getting to my mind dangerously near the creation of a slave state because he is saying that everything in this area or that must be subordinated to the goal. Of course you can talk about life, liberty and the pursuit of happiness but that is not a purpose in the managerial sense of the term. You cannot derive aims, objectives and operating plans from it. But on the other hand an enterprise can and normally does have objectives. It also normally has to have a *raison d'etre* which is not necessary for an individual and not thought to be required for a state. That is one of the big differences about enterprises; they can and frequently do, have overriding purposes, to which everything can be subordinated.

It has to be admitted, that enterprises and the general human organisation of people for the achievement of a purpose have produced absolutely incredible results. The power of an organisation to achieve a purpose is many, many times greater than the sum of the individual powers of the people comprising it. All we have as individuals is the same sort of muscles and brains that we had 2000 years ago; but put it all together in an organisation and the things than can be achieved are absolutely incredible, way beyond anything than an individual or even that particular collection of individuals could do unorganised. But they have to be organised. The common way of thinking about organisation is as a model of a human person with a head, a brain for direction, eyes and ears for information gathering, arms and legs for the motor parts of the organisation, the doing part of it, and we stitch all these together with a rough imitation of the central nervous system. We do not appear to know any other way of creating an organisation except on this anthropromorphic model. But one has to admit that this approach has worked wonders in terms of enormous changes in the environment. Whether for good or bad is another matter, but its power is absolutely undoubted.

We still use these anthropromorphic words, talking about people being at the head of an organisation. We have, however, given up advertising for 'hands' as we used to, which is a recognition that in the enterprise, in the same way as the state, people whose position is subordinate, are still nevertheless people and have to be treated not just as hands or brains or whatever, but as people. If you do not treat them as people they will rebel; and even if you do they will be slipping out from under you because the first thing to remember about any organisation is that it does not actually operate the way you think it does. The people who are doing the job, whether it is at the coal face or in the branch of a bank, are not actually doing what the book says they should. They may be achieving approximately the same result; frequently doing it better than the book says, but sometimes skipping it and doing it in a slip-shod way. But nevertheless they have adapted it to themselves, how they like to work, how they like to behave, how it looks to them and sometimes what they think the organisation wants. It can be quite different from what it really wants. So that just as the people in a state have a great capacity for getting out from under and finding ways round things so the people in an enterprise have an equal capacity for getting out from under and sorting things out to suit themselves.

My son went to work for a short time in an engineering works. He had acquired an extremely antique scooter and discovered that it would be perfectly normal for him to repair it, and in fact replace a good many of the parts, during the lunch hour using the firm's tools and a fair amount of its materials. If this encroached into the firm's time, as long as it was not too much, nobody bothered, since they were all doing it.

It is well known that in Birmingham nobody ever pays retail prices for engineering products. People just adapt themselves to the situation they are in. That is the number one thing to be remembered about any enterprise, about the relationship between the individual and the enterprise. In my opinion that is more fundamental than the fact that people have organised themselves into trade unions, so that they can use their power to bring pressure to bear on the employer to shift the direction of the enterprise for their own benefit.

I think there are a few cracks beginning to appear in the trade union clay too. Although it has not been said so much recently, with unemployment as high as it is, for a good many years after the war, when governments adopted policies of high employment and apparently successfully, a lot of chaps began to wonder why they were paying trade union subscriptions. Now in times of a wage freeze they are again beginning to wonder what they are paying trade union subscriptions for. The combination of that and other activities in the state has produced the phenomenum known as the 'lump', which is again the individual getting out from under and saying to hell with the trade union, the state, the Social Security, and if possible taxation too. I will become an entrepreneur of my own. Naturally there is an unholly alliance between the unions and the Inland Revenue to try to put down the 'lump'. In fact it is one of the greatest flowers of the human spirit to appear in the last few years, and there had better be more of it.

Now I do not think that the individual is eroding and attacking the enterprise in the way that he is eroding and attacking the state. Certainly he will, because that is the

nature of the individual, but there is no reason whatever in
my mind to think that an enterprise cannot cope with it,
because the benefits and the power that an enterprise can
bring are so great. Provided you realise that the mice in the
wainscot are the people on the payroll, and that has to be
recognised and coped with, then I think enterprises can
continue to flourish provided, of course, that the state
allows them to; and here I come to a relationship on which I
do not think I can be quite so optimistic.

The enterprise and the state

Consider the relationship between the state and enterprises,
that is to say most of the commercial and industrial
businesses. I can spend a very long time describing the sorry
state of that relationship since the end of the war. There
have been desperately serious mistakes on both sides, but I
will simply start from where we are now with what the
government calls its industrial strategy. There is the
National Economic Development Office, the two sides of
industry and there is the government with its forecasts for
next year and the next five years. Behind them there are
thirty-nine little NEDDYS. Everything is passed about to one
or the other — each of them three-fold, government,
unions and management. Each of them make their plans
for their industries or their sector. These are brought in, put
together and inconsistencies identified. Opportunities are
spotted, obstacles noted and messages go back and forth.
Then away everybody goes, with government help where it
is required. And there it is. If it worked at least it would be
coherent, in the way that a lot of the government activities
in this field up to now have not been coherent. We would
have taken a large step towards France, possibly overtaken
France and got three-quarters the way to Japan. There is
nothing particularly political in this and nothing Marxist at
all.

It really is to my mind an expression of what I said earlier — people looking for a substitute for war — 'let us make it international competition', 'let us build our army for the international trade battle and take on the Americans, the French, the Germans and the Japanese'. 'Let us get ourselves organised to do that.' This is the strongest attempt that I have seen to set up such an organisation, but it means, of course, the abandonment of the market concept at home. The international marketplace remains abroad, but at home it is virtually laid down in a plan. And I regret to say I think that the mice will get at that too. The individual will not stand for it. I cannot see it working and I am not altogether sure that I would like it to. But nevertheless that is the situation that I think we have reached or are about to reach in the relationship between the state and enterprises in Britain.

I think I have gone round the triangle now — individual, state and enterprise — and tried to be provocative at various points.

3 The National Enterprise Board

Lord Ryder

Lord Ryder of Eaton Hastings was appointed Industrial Adviser to the Government in 1974 and was subsequently appointed Chairman of the National Enterprise Board in November 1975. His wide business experience includes having been Director of the International Publishing Corporation, the Managing Director of the Reed Paper Group and Chairman and Chief Executive of Reed International Ltd. He is also a member of the British Gas Corporation, and serves on the Council of the British Institute of Management and the Court of Cranfield Institute of Technology.

The theme of this series of seminars has a rather philosophical ring about it and I hope this audience will forgive me, as an essentially practical businessman, for being somewhat fuller on practice than on philosophy. Having said that, I think that the creation of the National Enterprise Board does raise a number of issues that are relevant to your theme.

Of the three elements — the individual, the enterprise and the state — I shall in practice concentrate on the last two. That is not to say that the rights and needs of the individual have no bearing on the NEB and the companies it controls. On the contrary, we are expressly required under our guidelines from the government to ensure that the needs of consumers — which is one way of referring to the individual — are properly taken into account; and our largest subsidiary, British Leyland, is in the type of business where to ignore the wishes of the consumer — which means you or me — is a recipe for disaster.

I thought however, that it would be sensible to narrow down the theme somewhat to that of the relationship between government and industry, and to tackle it under three main headings: first, the general characteristics of government-industry relations; secondly, some observations on the main strategic issues which should influence industrial strategy in this country; and finally the role of the NEB.

It is often felt that the state interferes far too much in the affairs of industry — so much so that those vital ingredients of the Western economic system, initiative and enterprise, are in danger of being stifled. There is also a widespread feeling that this interference has been increasing more rapidly in recent years.

It is only natural to feel, every time there is some new kind of state intervention in industry, that it is appreciably more radical than anything that has gone before. But in the heat of the argument about government involvement in industry — which we all know tends to arouse strong and opposing passions — it is easy to overlook certain basic facts:

1 government involvement has been going on for a very long time;
2 it has been continued under successive governments of different political complexions;
3 it exists in varying degrees in most industrialised countries.

Arguments about government involvement in industry have been in progress in this country since the Industrial Revolution and indeed before that. Import duties are, after all, the classic example of intervention by government in the free flow of trade and the debate between those who want more of them and those who want less of them has been going on now for several centuries, right up to the Common Market referendum in 1975 and beyond.

I think it is possible to identify five or six main types of government involvement in industry in this country. The earliest was the concept of the government as regulator — providing ground rules for industrial and commercial behaviour on such matters as the maximum hours of work for children, the rights and obligations of a limited liability company, or the curbing of monopoly activities.

At the beginning of the Second World War, following the depression years of the 1930s, government assumed a new responsibility — that of trying to manage demand in the economy as a whole, according to Keynesian principles. At the end of the War came the third phase of government involvement in industry — the nationalisation of the basic industries concerned with energy and transportation.

In the early 1960s, under first a Conservative Government and then a Labour Government, there was a fourth type of government intervention — the attempt through national planning to generate a more rapid and more sustained rate of growth in the economy. Allied to that was the growing emphasis given to regional policies, which can be traced back to the 1930s but were given a significant boost in the 1960s.

Finally there has been the phase of selective government intervention in the affairs of particular companies and industries. An early example was the scheme of the early 1960s for rationalising and modernising the textile industry; but the phase perhaps began in earnest in the latter half of the 1960s with the creation of the Ministry of Technology and has continued under successive governments (both Conservative and Labour) and through various departmental reorganisations to the present day.

Experience in this country has certainly not been unique. In most industrialised countries government involvement in industry is considerable — even in countries such as the United States, West Germany and Japan, which we normally regard as examples of successful free enterprise rather than state controlled.

In the United States, anti-monopoly powers have tended to be applied with much greater rigour than here; there is a powerful network of regulatory public agencies; the award of military contracts has been an influential instrument of industrial planning; and the federal government has found itself drawn into giving guarantees for the Lockheed Aircraft Corporation and direct subsidies for passenger rail services.

If we look at the countries of the EEC, taking the crude ratio of state to private enterprise, we find Italy comfortably at the head of the league. Their state holding company, IRI, has obvious parallels with some of the functions of the NEB as does a similar state holding company, *Statsfoeretag*, in Sweden.

But merely looking at ownership neglects the more subtle and indirect ways in which state intervention, in the broadest sense, can occur. In West Germany, for instance, the government has pursued an active regional policy; and considerable indirect influence is brought to bear on industry through active management on the part of institutions, creditors and shareholders. And France, I believe, provides even more striking examples, and on a much larger scale.

If therefore we take a longer and wider perspective, looking backward at our own history or looking around us at what happens in other industrialised countries, there is no reason to suppose that there is anything fundamentally new or different about the forms of government involvement in industry which we find in Britain today. It is a situation which I believe we must accept as inevitable.

Most chief executives of companies probably wish at some time or another that they were back in the golden age when they could take straightforward business decisions without regard to the sticks and carrots with which they feel governments alternatively browbeat and cajole them. But that world, if it ever existed, has gone forever. A modern industrialised economy is no longer that simple, elegant, self-regulating machine which the classical economists constructed. Like most devices of the modern world, it is extremely clever and complex and it is apt to go wrong at inconvenient moments. And when that happens people are not prepared to see the government which they elect stand idly by.

My conclusion therefore is that a close relationship between government and industry in this country is both necessary and inevitable. But the kind of close relationship which exists at present leaves a good deal of room for improvement.

A lot of the trouble lies in certain traditional differences of attitude. Some businessmen, as I indicated earlier, think that the state ought to keep out of industry and let them get on with their job of creating the nation's wealth. Some politicians and civil servants, on the other hand, suspect that industry's horizons can be too narrow — that decisions may be taken for short-term commercial reasons and that the results of these decisions, in aggregate, can be detrimental not only to industry itself but to the nation as a whole.

I have the strong impression that in other countries this relationship, even where it is just as close, if not closer, tends to be more co-operative. I suspect this is because government-industry relations in this country have tended to be politicised here much more than in most other Western countries. I would like to see us move towards a more stable relationship which combines the right sort of scope for government to exercise its responsibilities for the national economy with scope for industry to display its talents of initiative and enterprise.

The building of this relationship will have to be a long and patient process. It will need to include the following main ingredients.

On industry's part there should be a keener recognition of its wider responsibilities. Both the CBI and many individual firms have, I know, done a great deal in recent years to define a company's responsibilities, not just to its shareholders but also to its workers, to the nation and to society. But traditional attitudes die hard and we have a long way to go yet.

On the government's part there should be a more strategic and less detailed approach to control and intervention, both in the publicly-owned and in the privately-owned sectors of industry. The discussion of forward plans and annual budgets can provide the basis for this: once these are agreed, the government should try as far as possible to refrain from further short-term interference.

The approach to industrial strategy which is being developed under the aegis of the National Economic Development Council gives me some grounds for encouragement. The original policy statement by the government in November 1975 set the tone: the intention was 'to give greater weight, and more consistently than hitherto, to the need for increasing the national rate of growth through regenerating our industrial structure and improving efficiency'.

The most important thing is that we now have some objectives for industrial policy which are related to practical realities, not to some grandiose notion of national planning of the 1960s variety. It is vital that we continue to work toward these objectives; for without a soundly-based strategy for industry, the new policy instruments introduced by the Industry Act 1975 — which include the NEB — will be largely ineffective. It is therefore worth considering the most important elements of such a strategy and how the NEB can contribute to their achievement.

Fundamental to any industrial strategy must be the defeat of inflation — so fundamental that I need merely to mention it in order to leave it on one side. The key elements of a sound strategy then seem to me to fall into five main categories, each of which is recognised to a greater or lesser extent in the Neddy work. They are:

1 Better co-ordination of government policies affecting industry and a more stable and satisfactory climate for industrial activity;

2 More effective use of policy instruments specifically directed at industry;

3 Ensuring that sufficient finance is available to industry both in the form of internally generated profits and from external sources;

4 More effective use of manpower, including training and re-training and encouragement of improved productivity;

5 Improved planning by all parties resulting from a tripartite approach, in which management, labour and Government each makes a contribution.

The NEB has a part to play in nearly all of these aspects of industrial strategy, and at this point it might help if I were to remind you of the main functions of the Board.

The NEB is, first and foremost, a new source of investment capital for industry. It draws the bulk of its funds from the government, but it is not a government department. It is a public corporation, with its own Board, and therefore has to make its own decisions and stand by their consequences.

The objectives of the NEB are written into the Industry Act 1975 and include the assisting of the economy of the UK, promoting industrial efficiency and international competitiveness, and providing support for productive employment. Its emphasis will be on improving the performance of key sectors of manufacturing industry.

Its functions fall under three main headings:-

1 A new source of finance for industrial development. The NEB's role is to supplement, not to displace, the supply of investment from existing sources, and it aims to draw its customers primarily from manufacturing concerns with good long-term potential but with a need to embark on substantial programmes of modernisation and re-equipment. Most finance will therefore tend to be in the form of equity participation, but the NEB is also able to make loans.

2 Like the former Industrial Reorganisation Corporation, the NEB can act as a catalyst in helping to bring about rationalisation or restructuring of key sectors of industry — either by providing finance or by acting in an advisory capacity.

3 The NEB is a new kind of publicly-owned industrial enterprise, whose function is that of a holding company for a number of companies, such as British Leyland and Rolls-Royce (1971), in which the

government in some cases previously held the shares. This function has several counterparts abroad, for example, in Sweden, France and Italy, as I mentioned earlier. The holdings will be added to from time to time, both as a result of the investment financing activities and also through purchases of existing shares under precisely the same arrangements that apply to companies trading in the private sector. The size of new holdings, and the degree of control that goes with them, depend on the circumstances of the particular case.

In all these activities the NEB has an explicit duty to see that its investments earn an adequate return. Unlike most nationalised industries, it does not have a monopoly in any particular product. NEB companies have to compete in world markets.

The NEB also has to abide by all the rules that apply in the private sector — for example, on fair trading policy, the City takeover code, and pay policy. And it has an obligation to ensure that the taxpayers, who are in a sense the NEB's shareholders, get the best possible return. If these duties are to be fulfilled, it is obviously desirable that the government should leave the NEB free, as far as possible, from day-to-day interferences — especially since the NEB's position as a holding company responsible for a wide range of manufactured products puts it in a class apart not only from the traditional, public utility type of nationalised industry but also, I would suggest, from a body like the British Steel Corporation.

Let me now outline how I see the NEB contributing to the various key elements of industrial strategy which I listed earlier.

First, better co-ordination of government policies affecting industry. Obviously this is something on which the government itself must take the lead. But one of the reasons why policies are not always as well co-ordinated as they might be is that, as I have suggested, government-industry relations tend to be conducted in an atmosphere of mutual suspicion, aggravated sometimes by political attitudes.

There is also, as I suggested earlier, a crying need for more stability and for a greater measure of bi-partisan agreement on industrial policy. The country needs continuity of policies, which requires that the major parties consult on areas which have a fundamental bearing on the success of the country's economic future. The lack of stable industrial policy followed by successive governments has done untold damage to the country. Policies have been reversed by successive governments even where these were clearly policies which should have been maintained in the national interest. Many people would say that the winding up of the IRC was a case in point.

As for the NEB, it is very much to be hoped that our politicians will judge it strictly on its merits and on its performance. Provided that we acquit ourselves well, it is hard to see why there should not be a consensus at least on the need for an independent agency like the NEB, not subject to day-to-day government control, with the task of providing overall direction to those companies in the public sector which have to compete with the world at large. It is worth remembering that Rolls-Royce for example, was brought into public ownership by a Conservative Government, while British Leyland was brought into public ownership by a Labour Government.

If the position of the NEB in the armoury of industrial policy instruments is assured, I believe that it can do a lot to help improve relations between government and industry.

In a sense it holds the ring between them. It is a completely new body; it is neither a hived-off part of the civil service nor an existing commercial organisation brought into public ownership. It inherits no traditions, no fixed ways of thinking, and no prejudices or preconceptions. It has complete freedom to recruit and develop the skills it needs for its operations. As an essentially entrepreneurial body, the NEB will be looking to the private sector for most of these skills. But at the same time will take particular care to ensure that they are tempered with an understanding of the peculiar problems that exist at the interface between government and industry.

Next let us consider how the NEB can help to make specific instruments of government industrial policy more effective. The NEB is itself one of those instruments, and it is obviously in the NEB's interest to help to see that its activities contribute fully to the government's industrial strategy.

Naturally the NEB will be keeping in close touch with the outcome of the work of identifying key sectors of manufacturing industry for priority treatment. It will try always, other things being equal, to ensure that its programme of investments reflects the same priorities that are agreed in tripartite discussions at national level. It will also be on the lookout for situations where worthwhile projects can go ahead with the aid of suitable government incentives as well as NEB finance.

Thirdly, there is the need to ensure that adequate funds are available for productive investment. Obviously in purely financial terms the NEB's resources are small compared with the funds available to industry from other sources. But we have a distinctive contribution to make. For example, we shall be pursuing a policy of positive and active investment management: if our investments do not produce results, we shall take more constructive action than merely voting with our feet. We shall be asking the management of the company some searching questions.

Again, we shall always be on the lookout for situations where timely intervention can prevent a company from getting into the kind of state where only drastic action can save it. But NEB intervention will have relatively little impact if the private sector does not play its part too. As a convinced supporter of the mixed economy — by which I mean an economy where there is genuine, healthy competition between the public and private sectors — I naturally welcome the initiative of the City in setting up Equity Capital for Industry, with objectives very similar to those of the NEB. Of course it always has to be recognised that writing out a cheque is not enough if it is not followed up by proper monitoring of performance. This is what I mean by positive and active investment management.

Then there is the question of manpower policy. This again is something in which the government must take the lead. But the NEB can reinforce it in three ways. First, the NEB will be looking for every opportunity to improve the quality of the management of companies in which it has an interest, by seeking out and promoting younger talent. I believe there are enormous gains to be had from releasing the energy and ideas of our middle managers in industry. Secondly and complementary to the first task the NEB will be looking for ways of stimulating various forms of worker participation in decision-making, the success of which abroad, particularly as a way of enhancing productivity, is now coming to be recognised increasingly in this country. It is a task with which the NEB is explicitly charged under the Industry Act. Thirdly the NEB will always give priority, other things being equal, to investments which have a significant effect in maintaining or augmenting productive employment, especially in the areas of high unemployment.

Finally, there is the tripartite spirit. I need hardly say that this is absolutely fundamental to the NEB's relations with its companies. It is no longer a political issue — it is a fact of life, amply borne out by recent experience, that policies of confrontation of 'them and us', are a recipe for disaster. Industry cannot hope to succeed without the closest possible co-operation and consultation between all parties concerned — management, trade unions and government.

The NEB would be failing in its duty if it did not do everything in its power to help to cement that relationship.

To conclude, let me express the hope that we might get away from talking about 'intervention' and 'interference', and think of it more as co-operation and partnership between industry and government. All industrialists I am sure want to see this country get back into the top league and I am no exception. But we cannot hope to achieve this unless we carry the government along with us. That is one of the reasons why I took the step — which I believe was a completely rational one — of leaving a highly successful and profitable company in the private sector to help set up the NEB.

I am convinced that the NEB has an essential part to play in helping and strengthening industry; and I am encouraged by what I have seen so far to believe that industry will increasingly respond in a fashion which will enable us to play that part.

4 A political angle

Mr. Dick Taverne Q.C.

Introducing Mr. Taverne, the Centre's Director pointed out how admirably his career spanned the theme of the seminar: 'At the level of the state, he was for some ten years Labour member for Lincoln, holding various ministerial posts including Secretary to the Treasury. At the level of the enterprise he is currently a non-executive director of BOC International, an appointment which takes a lot of his time; he is on the Board of Equity and Law Insurance and is also Director of the Institute for Fiscal Studies. As for his interests in the individual and the balance between the three, his own particular interests lie in creating a new political alignment of the Centre. The formation of the Social Democratic Party and his return as Member for Lincoln in 1973 is well known.'

Mr. Taverne is an Oxford graduate of Balliol College, and was President of the Oxford Union in 1951.

I notice that in the list of speakers contributing to this series, there are no other politicians. I am not in politics now but I have been in government and I did spend about thirteen years in Parliament. So I want to approach this topic from the political angle and to look mainly at the role of government. It is not an easy task. The extent of the role of the state goes to the heart of political philosophy and practising politicians or formerly practising politicians make bad philosophers; but I hope to stick to a severely practical approach. All parties now accept a substantial role for the state, some more than others. For the purposes of this talk I shall assume that we accept a mixed economy and I will ignore, for our purposes, the arguments of contemporary Marxists that the role of the state should be greatly extended in the management of the economy. I say contemporary Marxists because while contemporary Marxists want to see a vast extension of public ownership, it is not something that Marx himself discussed at great length.

In the late 1950s, the philosopher on the left who exercised the greatest influence on social democrats like myself was Tony Crosland. On the one hand he mounted a pretty devastating attack on the Marxists who argued that only through a state owned economy could a more just society be created and on the other hand he argued that a civilised society demanded a high level of public spending and would therefore have to accept a high level of taxation. His views were reinforced by Galbraith with his denunciation of public squalor amid private affluence and, broadly speaking, it was this kind of approach which dominated the moderates in the Labour government between '64 and '70. Indeed they dominate the views of the moderates, or at least the aspirations of the moderates, in the present Government; and were also reflected, perhaps to a lesser extent, in the policies of the Heath Government after its initial Selsden stage. It helped ministers like Keith

Joseph and Margaret Thatcher, in health and education respectively, to boast of their achievements in increasing the proportions of the GNP which was spent on their departments.

Now there has been a reaction against the Crosland viewpoint. It has not only come from the Conservative right but also from Social Democrats like Roy Jenkins. Indeed the official policy of the present Government, as declared in the statements of the Prime Minister and the Chancellor, is to reduce the share of the national wealth taken by public spending over the next few years. The argument in the Cabinet about cuts at the present time is perhaps a temporary diversion, being not so much an argument about the total role of public spending as an argument about what should be done at the moment when nobody knows where we are.

I believe that we may well have reached the high water mark of the role of the state and I think to Social Democrats as well as others, the Crosland approach is out of date. The case for higher public spending is no longer convincing and there are, to my mind, three reasons why this is so, all of which are more or less relevant to the theme of these lectures. The first is economic, which I do not wish to spend much time on but is obviously one which cannot be ignored. Theoretically there is no reason why high spending and high taxation should necessarily inhibit economic growth, indeed there are countries which have a higher rate of economic growth than we have which have as high a rate of public spending and a higher proportion of their total wealth taken in taxes. It is a myth that we are the most heavily taxed nation in Europe. Nevertheless there is little doubt that the government's borrowing requirement is one of the greatest obstacles to the restoration of economic prosperity or to economic recovery. It is also quite clear that the government cannot, in present circumstances, increase taxes to meet the level of its spending, whilst at the same time the gap between the two is one of the main causes of inflation and lack of confidence abroad and in business at home. I do not believe that any economically literate member of the Cabinet, of the present Cabinet, would now defend the enormous increases in public spending which took place in 1974. They were warned, some of them realised the danger, most of them felt that they had to persist because of circumstances beyond their control but at least they have repented.

Now we are not in this series primarily concerned with economics. In some ways a more fundamental objection to the high level of public spending is that it has not achieved its original aims and has not benefitted the individuals in the way which was intended. Politicians are very prone to the quantitative fallacy. When the days of a general election approach, the defending party spends a great deal of time reeling off statistics on public platforms which suggest the success of the outgoing administration — look how many houses we have built, look how many schools we have built, look how much extra we have spent on welfare, look how many bills we have passed through Parliament. Somehow it seems to be a test of the political virility of administrations to point to the amount of legislation that they have passed. I think it is fair to say that Harold Wilson was the champion *par-excellance* in this approach, just as he cited the number of ministers he had appointed, so he cited the number of laws he had passed to show that Britain was a better place.

Now I think few people stop to ask what the extra spending has actually achieved. At least until recently they did not do so. Have the extra thousands of millions which are now spent on housing compared with ten years ago actually reduced the number of homeless? Has the enormous rise in the share of the national wealth to which successive ministers of education have been able to point actually improved the quality of education? Has the increase in spending on the Health Service actually improved the nation's health? In fact has this huge rise in public spending of the kind which Crosland advocated, and in which many people like myself strongly believed, in fact made Britain a more civilised place?

If one starts to examine the results in terms of achievement, or of justice, or of greater equality of opportunity, it is by no means clear that more has meant better. There is a considerable body of evidence, not perhaps conclusive, but *prima facie* convincing, that standards of literacy have dropped; and examiners are finding that the standards of those taking 'O' levels and 'A' levels are lower than they were before. Perversely it seems the more we have spent the less we have promoted the equality of opportunity to which all our efforts are devoted. The high increase in housing subsidies has not lessened the number of homeless. It is doubtful whether in recent times the standards of service in the Health Service have improved and yet the spending on it has increased not just in absolute terms but relative to the proportion of GNP. The vast increase of spending on the social services since the Seebohm Report has not, as far as one can see, improved the services to the deprived; there is much evidence that it has made them more remote. The railways and the bus services cost the tax payer more, while their service to passengers has declined; and as the standards decline the demand for spending increases. One could almost derive from all this a kind of principle of perversity that what you legislate for has the opposite effect to what is intended. ·

Indeed one can cite a large number of statutes which have done this very thing. Rent control, designed to protect tenants, has not meant security of tenure but no tenure for some hundreds of thousands. The Protection of Employment Act, designed to protect employment, is likely to freeze the existing pattern of employment more than it would do otherwise and will possibly make long-term unemployment worse. The Prices Code enables many

people to raise their prices. This is a paradoxical statement
but I have found it to be true in practice; since one can
prove a legal price increase and many customers seem to
have accepted these, because they are legal, where otherwise
they might have refused. I could multiply many examples of
how legislation has in fact defeated its own ends. Where
have we gone wrong?

It is not as if the critique of high spending only comes
from the right. Many of the criticisms made by Milton
Friedman are echoed in the writings of Ivan Illich, from a
very different angle but often tending to the same
conclusions. And one does not have to be a Friedmanite to
see that much of the demand for an expansion of state
services comes from within the machine. It is after all
natural. If you are an educational administrator you are
constantly faced with problems, for example over-sized
classes. How do you solve it? You call for more teachers.
You hear about the old school buildings; so how do you
solve it? You call for more spending on new school
buildings. Every administrator can see weaknesses in the
service he provides and finds the answer in spending more
money. By the very nature of his job, the public servant is
unlikely to search for radical and quite different
alternatives. So the Department of the Environment pushes
the road programme even more strongly than the
motoring organisations.

Wherever you look it is the government which presses for
more spending rather than the public. It is the government
which identifies needs rather than demands. Needs I should
say are demands which the government feels ought to be
made as compared with what the public wants. After a
time however the government is just as successful in
creating demands as advertising was in the very convincing
argument of Galbraith in creating demands for the
products of private enterprise. So public spending grows
and grows, yet the service that it offers does not seem to

satisfy the individuals for whose benefits it was intended. Indeed I think it is true to say on general observation that discontent increases with the level of expenditure.

There is, however, a third reason for opposing the high level of public spending and the expanding role for government. This is where it limits the role of the individual. I see nothing radical, democratic or socially progressive in creating a centrally administrative bureaucracy which dispenses, on an ever increasing scale, welfare, health, education, housing and jobs to a public of passive recipients who become less independent as the dispensation increases in scale.

Most people do not like receiving charity if they can help it. Most people are happier if they can keep themselves healthy and become independent of medical services. Parents prefer to choose schools which provide the kind of education they want rather than what the government decides is good for their children. Most people given the choice and the means would rather live in their own house, even if they have to do their own repairs rather than depend on the efficiency of the council. As for jobs most people seem happiest working for themselves or at any rate in surroundings where they know the people they work with or work for. In large organisations the happiest employees seem to be found where the individual subsidiary unit is small and largely independent; and I understand that amongst personnel relations experts it is a truism that the problems of industrial relations multiply with the size of the factory or plant.

Now what moral can we derive from this analysis of the role of the state? That governments should not seek to do too much. If it does it will increase our economic problems, fail to achieve its social aims and lessen the scope for individual self-expression. Our basic principle should therefore be that government should only do what the individual cannot do for himself. Perhaps it can be re-stated in the form that central government should not do what local government can do just as well and that local government should not do what the individual can do for himself.

The same principle could well be extended to private enterprises; they should not do centrally what can be done locally.

Now if this principle is followed then it seems likely that the services provided would be more efficient. There is plenty of evidence, from education for example, that government is at least twice as inefficient as the private sector in providing the service. In private schools I have looked at, the ratio of administrators to teachers has varied from 1 to 5 to 1 to 10. In the Inner London Education Authority there are more administrators than teachers. The dis-economies of scale are huge.

Now this does not immediately entail a stampede into the philosophical camp of Mrs. Thatcher and Keith Joseph. (It should be mentioned as I indicated earlier that this refers to Mrs. Thatcher and Keith Joseph, Mark II, because Mark I was on view in the period 1971 to 1973 and no wonder Mr. Heath got somewhat annoyed.) People take very different views of what the individual can achieve for himself or what other forces can threaten his independence. Conservatives, in my view, are rightly suspicious about the magnificent effects of state activity. They are surprisingly uncritical at times about the effects of leaving large or not so large corporations unaccountable. If the individual is to have the chance to express himself and to realise his full potential, someone must watch the tendency for power to concentrate in a very few hands. If the power of the king is controlled the citizen needs protection from the barons. Sometimes this means restoring some power to the king. The state has a vital regulatory function to perform which no-one else can adequately fulfil, provided that its exercise is subject to the basic principle of minimal intervention. Personally I also believe that certain services can only be adequately provided to those whom birth or other accidents have placed at a special disadvantage if government supplies the finance. Several vital functions cannot be performed by commercial organisations.

Now there are obvious examples of this. One is anti-monopoly legislation. It is a good example of the need for powers of the king to curb the barons. One important question, to my mind a central question, is this: 'If the barons nevertheless, even when there is anti-monopoly legislation, exercise great powers over individuals, is there not also a need for accountability and does this not justify state ownership?' I accept the need for accountability, I think there must always be some limit on arbitrary power. I do not, however, accept that in most cases central accountability can be effective. I think one of the great problems which radicals and others face in politics today is what form of accountability can be most effective.

All our experience shows that when it comes to central accountability the large public corporations are no more accountable to the public than the large private corporations. Parliament cannot control them. It is completely incapable of controlling any administration in its present form, but it would be the wrong body in any event to control a large commercial operation, even if it was reformed. Attempts by the government machine itself to exercise control on our behalf have increased inefficiency and added to bureaucracy. We must look for different solutions.

Now accountability should, I think, be sought on a smaller and more effective scale. One way lies through workshop democracy, the works councils which function extremely well on the whole in Germany and Holland, and in many British companies, where those who work in an enterprise share power over the environment in which they work and are involved through representatives whom they know and see every day. On the Continent they have found that this form of democracy is enhanced by a reform of company structure with the representation of employees on the supervisory board. But they have not found that the second representation on the board is any substitute for the first which is the democracy in the workshop. I am disturbed by suggestions that we will see the board representation and not necessarily the extension of the local works councils. Board representatives could soon become remote. The union leaders who find the places on the board are likely to be less in touch with the needs and feelings of most workers on the shop floor than good managers in a well run factory. But unfortunately if the motto is to be 'More Power to the Union' then developments may take place which prejudice the vertical democracy which I think is more important and which, of course, conflicts with the horizontal level on which the unions' power is based.

Another form of accountability lies in the maximum transparency of the operations of an enterprise. The more the consumer and the local community, the employees, the customer, and where appropriate the government, can be told about the aims and methods and achievements of a company the greater the control which those who are effected by a company's activities have over it. Indirectly, knowledge is power. Openness of operations is a form of accountability. It has, of course, to be remembered that not everything can be revealed and that commercial secrets must be preserved from competitors.

A third form of accountability, in which I am most interested, lies in the real de-centralisation of the activities of the enterprise and particularly of those run by the state itself. Services provided by government enterprises, whether through central or local government, are in practice less accountable most of the time than those of the private sector. Many private commercial companies operate much more openly than nationalised concerns. But I have also mentioned earlier the desire of parents for choice of schools. Many of us accept that education is one of the activities which must be provided by the state perhaps not exclusively but certainly for the majority. At the same time it does not, as presently organised, offer sufficient choice or influence for parents. It is a classic case of the diseconomies of scale.

Why not let the state finance local schools but give them a measure of independence so that they can be run by teachers in consultation with parents? Why have the large bureaucratic machine of the county educational department at all? State finance need not necessarily imply detailed control. We have seen that in universities through the model of the University Grants Commission.

Why not cut out the intermediate layer of organisation in the Health Service and give financial autonomy, provided with state funds, to local hospitals so that they can use the funds as they, that is the doctors, nurses and the local representatives of the patients (which from practice would be councillors) think best? A greater degree of local independence would certainly create a degree of financial responsibility which is often absent in the administration of a hospital. It might also involve the medical service more closely in the life of the community and might spur us to look more closely at prevention than we do today.

In each case the state would continue to provide certain central services which cannot be run locally. In education the state would provide the universities and perhaps certain specialist schools. In health it would provide teaching hospitals and other forms of special treatment. I offer these suggestions not as blue-prints. The particular proposals may not work but they do indicate the lines on which the principle of minimal intervention might be implemented.

My theme has been to emphasise the desire for organisation on the smallest possible scale. It is worth stressing that I do not imagine naively that small is always beautiful. I do not imagine that every enterprise, state or private, can be de-centralised, nor that somehow or other we will find scope for steel plants as a cottage industry or for the small-scale manufacture of jumbo jets. Nor should one imagine that small-scale activity is inevitably beneficial in the environment sense. The Sahara and many other wastes were almost certainly created by localised, de-centralised private enterprise activities. Nevertheless we do, I suspect, need to think again about the ideal size of the environment in which most people work and in which they have an opportunity to express themselves.

We should realise, on the Left as well as on the Right, that the greatest threat to the ideal of people controlling and influencing their own lives, lies in the power of central government.

5 The primacy of the individual

Mr. Jacques G. Maisonrouge

Mr. Maisonrouge has been Chairman and Chief Executive of IBM Europe/Middle East/Africa Corporation since 1974 and a Director of IBM United Kingdom Holdings since 1971. He studied engineering and gained the Diploma of the Ecole Central des Arts et Manufactures. He has held various appointments in IBM Corporation, France and IBM World Trade Corporation.

I am delighted to be here with you today in this environment. It is a pleasure to step back, catch one's breath, and consider some of the issues inherent in the relationship between the individual, the enterprise, and the state. I am going to be philosophic, but I will try to be concise. The other day, the London *Times* had a story about how an Appeals Court reversed a sentence because the trial judge's three-day summation literally 'bored the jury to sleep'. The Appeals Court termed the judge 'excessively conscientious'. I aim for a more attentive jury today, and I do hope that your judgement will be less severe. The topic excites me because, as it is phrased, it recognises that the individual comes first — before the enterprise and the state. That order coincides precisely with my own view.

My particular vantage point is one of a Frenchman sitting in the European headquarters of a multinational company based in the United States. It is a position that has enabled me to observe the relationships between the individual, business, and the state in a number of cultural contexts. The experience has convinced me that, if these relationships are to be healthy so that each benefits from them, we have to get back to the basic recognition that all our structures exist to aid the individual. Or, as HRH Prince Philip recently put it in an address, 'We must get it firmly fixed in our minds that all the trappings of our social, religious, political and industrial systems exist for the sole purpose of allowing life to be as tolerable and as civilized as possible for the individual and the family'.

My own thesis stems directly from that premise. First, in a system based on the individual, the relationship between the state and the enterprise will depend on the individual's perception of his or her relationship with the enterprise. Second, if we truly believe in the primacy of the individual, then our goal should be to assure the proper functioning of the free enterprise system, which is the only system that puts the individual first. Third, by creating rapport in which the individual senses a commonality of interest with the enterprise and the state, we create true community out of a mass of individuals. Certainly, it is facile to talk about the primacy of the individual. And, certainly, that central goal can be too easily overlooked.

I will give you a concrete example from my own work. At IBM Europe in Paris, we have 1500 individuals backing up 82 country organisations in Europe, the Middle East and Africa. Just a few years ago, we started up this headquarters on a very small scale, in which good human relations was something of a natural byproduct. But we took that for granted and, as we grew, we realized that the human element was taking second place to the pressures of daily decision-making. People felt less in touch with top management and their comprehension of their contribution to their organisation suffered. We launched a programme aimed at giving the individual an understanding of his or her role in the enterprise and re-establishing the quality of human relationships that existed when our headquarters were smaller.

There are two keys to this programme. One is simply increasing human contact between departmental top managers and every one of the employees in their group so that everyone understands clearly the objectives and policies of the company. A second is two-way communication, in which employees meet with the top headquarters executives to discuss frankly goals and any questions or concerns. These kinds of meetings have been successful when IBM tried them in other units. People reported that their work had more meaning and they had more confidence in themselves to solve their own problems.

In fact, the programme simply re-emphasised the core of IBM personnel policies. That is 'respect for the individual'. The phrase may sound a bit statuesque, but underlying it is the same conviction that, in all of our relationships, the individual *must* come first.

Indeed, it is one of four basic beliefs at IBM which set the style for our company in its relationships with its various constituencies — employees, customers, stockholders and the societies in which we do business. In addition to 'respect to the individual' which has guided relationships with employees, we uphold three other basic beliefs:

The best service available to customers
Excellence in all undertakings
And corporate responsibility to
 society at large.

These are not just slogans. We back them up in everything we do. For example, respect for the individual means treating individual employees with dignity. That is reflected in our 'full employment' practice where we do everything possible to prevent economic crises or technological changes from affecting our employment levels. During the recent recession, we did not lay off a single individual. We shifted work to even out workloads and, in cases where manpower was simply too great to be accommodated, we provided education to enable individuals to learn new skills for new positions, very often involving promotions. This is expensive, but it is well worth it. In the last months I have had several occasions to discuss our full employment practice with many groups and, each time someone said 'You do it because you are a rich company', I had to explain every time that Mr. T.J. Watson Sr, the founder of our company, instituted this practice in the early thirties, at the time of the great depression in the United States, when IBM was a small company with heavy debts. The individual understands we mean it when we say that we value his or her contribution. In this way, the nature of the relationship between the individual and the enterprise takes on the sense of a community, a commonality of interest and purpose. That, I think, is the key to guaranteeing that the partners in the relationship gain from each other's contribution.

This policy of respect for the individual is also evident in our appraisal and counselling procedure. Each year, the employee and his or her manager sit down to discuss the year's work and jointly chart goals for the individual's career path including specific expectations for the next year. This is the kind of cooperation that I do not hesitate to term 'participation' in its fullest sense. It is a participation that gives maximum freedom to the individual to speak for himself or herself and jointly to make the decisions that most directly affect his or her future.

I believe that it is actually in the nature and quality of the relationship between the individual and the enterprise that one finds determined the essence of the relationship between the enterprise and the state. That is because in democratic societies, the political process should reflect the demands of the individual. If the individual is being treated unfairly by the enterprise, he will be signalling his representatives that government action is needed to straighten out the problem. Fair treatment of individuals should gain government approbation.

Indeed, I can present some empirical evidence on that score. During the 1975 recession, IBM's full employment practice was particularly valued — not only by individual employees but by governments. You can imagine how good I felt, for example, when the *New York Times* quoted a French government official as saying 'IBM's record in France is perfect'. That is the kind of comment that we are seeing more of, now that rational, impartial analysis of the role of the multinational enterprise is replacing the first emotional, uninformed allegations.

When I speak of the relationship between enterprise and society depending on the rapport between the individual and the enterprise, I am not only talking about the relationship between the enterprise and the employee. The state-business relationship also turns on the rapport between the customer and the enterprise. The customer's voice as an individual should have just as much weight as the employee's voice in determining government treatment of the enterprise.

This is where the nature of our product and service comes in. I believe that one reason why IBM is welcomed in so many countries is the contribution that its products make to customers, and to society as a whole. Data processing and word processing have been helping to boost productivity and fight inflation. These techniques have also improved jobs by removing some of the drudgery. We are happy with these results — and so are the customers and the societies they serve. Our challenge now is to make sure that fast-changing technology continues to be integrated comfortably and beneficially into society.

So the state's relationship with the enterprise will be based on judgements of employees and customers. But it will also turn on a third judgement — how the enterprise fits into the entire social context. That is where our belief on good corporate citizenship comes in.   .

Our actions back up this belief. IBM is often cited as an example of how multinationals can contribute to the counties in which they do business. For example, placing our plant in Greenock aided regional development goals of the government. We have also been credited with helping to stop the 'brain drain' by maintaining development laboratories in many countries. One impressive statistic I recently learned is that fifteen full professors in European universities are 'graduates' from our Zurich research lab. We operate seven European scientific centres that are using computers to address problems of society at large. Our scientific centre at Peterlee, for instance, is aiding municipal management of budgets and education through computer techniques. A centre in Italy has studied EEC economic modelling. And a centre in Madrid is analysing earth satellite photos to map Spanish mineral sources.

Our contributions to society go beyond application of our product. In London, two IBM projects are channeling business assistance to community groups and vocational training to teenagers. And at our International Education Centre near Brussels, two of our employees are teaching computer programming to handicapped students. The students will be guaranteed jobs in business when they graduate. Indeed, good corporate citizenship to IBM means meeting — and going beyond — the strict legal requirements of doing business. For example, when a 1971 French law required firms to spend one per cent of their payrolls on continuing education for their employees, IBM France was already spending 9.4 per cent. We have also gone beyond legal requirements to save energy and assure that IBM does not adversely affect the environment. In two years, we have cut fuel use twenty-seven per cent and electricity sixteen per cent. IBM Europe alone is spending about ten million pounds per year during this decade to assure environmental protection. At our Greenock plant, for example, we are going to be re-cycling freon and copper.

In the past few years, we have witnessed a great debate over the relationships between multinational firms and governments. At the outset, there were undocumented charges that the firms escaped government controls. Critics generalised on the base of a few examples where some firms did behave badly. Fortunately, we now have the benefit of impartial surveys, which show the positive contribution which large international firms make to societies and how the companies really are under strict government controls. A wide-ranging US Senate investigation concluded: 'In general, foreign suspicions that the multinational corporations are not accountable to host-country governments have found few grounds for validation in actual multinational corporation performance'.

Other surveys have shown how not even the largest corporations have escaped confiscatory measures of the smallest states and how many countries dictate production and export terms to foreign firms with local facilities. The recent OECD guidelines on MNCs implicitly acknowledge that governments have discriminated against foreign-based firms. These guidelines also set out codes of behaviour for business. Curiously, IBM's own code of business ethics could have served as a model for the OECD guidelines. Our code has been in place for decades now.

As you may recall, the OECD guidelines for international firms result from the past few years' debate over the role of MNCs in societies. As a keen observer of this debate, I must say that some of it was intellectually dishonest. Critics confused abuses of the free enterprise system with the system itself, just as I believe we wrongly blame the capitalist system for the results of industrialisation itself. If there are attacks against the free enterprise system, it is because it is not working the way it should, and not because the system itself is faulty. Criticism of bribery, corruption and unfair trading are not attacks on the system; they are attacks on abuses of *any* system. They have no part to play in the free enterprise system. The sooner that it is made clear, the healthier this system will be. And the more the public will appreciate it for what it really is.

For it seems to me that if the public really compared the results of political and economic systems, there would be a clear-cut decision to work to reform our current system instead of flirting with the idea of replacing it. For the fact is, the free enterprise system has not only brought more material benefits to more people than any other, but is also the system upon which the fullest array of true individual freedoms can be safeguarded. If we truly believe in the primacy of the individual at the base of our social, political and economic systems, then we must see to it that the free enterprise system is healthy. For the freedom of an individual to launch a business or pursue a trade of his free choice is an essential individual freedom that incorporates, as it defends, the exercise of other liberties.

I do not think we would entertain for one instant the idea that the state should dictate individual expression in writing or speaking or worship. Do we really wish to deny individual expression through curtailing opportunities to create an enterprise? Do we want to stop people from trying out improvements? Do we want to halt an individual when he takes personal risks to create goods and services demanded by others — and create jobs at the same time?

I know that critics say that the system is not working, that needs are 'created' and our wants manipulated. I do not believe that. All you need to do is look at studies like the American survey which showed that during one year thirty per cent of the products launched on the marketplace failed because they were rejected by the public. Another bit of evidence that the customer is still king is available from France today. Food distributors say that consumer rejection of products with artificial colouring has so affected sales that they are being forced to cut back on this practice.

Do we really want to limit a person's opportunity to better himself? I cannot believe that. We have seen how the free enterprise system has worked as such an equaliser, in spreading wealth and creating a middle class out of the huge gap between the hereditary rich and the poor.

This equaliser, I should add, has worked two ways — through rewards for risk-taking and performance and through return on invested capital of millions of stockholders. One of the great myths of our time is that dividends go to a small number of wealthy people and that these dividends are very substantial. In fact, in the US alone, about twenty-five million individuals hold stock in their own names. More millions are indirect owners through pension funds and life insurance, and dividends represent only five to eight per cent of the amounts distributed in salaries. Another myth concerns the profile of businessmen. A survey country showed that sixty per cent of businessmen were from modest or rural backgrounds.

Do we really want to limit hope? That is really what the defense of free enterprise comes to. And I am not being idealistic. If we compared the resignation of individuals in communist bloc countries with the forward-looking outlook of individuals in democratic nations with free enterprise, it is clear to me where I would want my children and grandchildren to face the future. I would want them in a country where they would be free to launch new ideas and have their countrymen judge their merits for themselves. To my mind, that is an essential condition for individual freedom.

There is one additional reason today to cherish the system of free enterprise. It is that in an era of fast technological change, we should encourage risk-taking and experimentation more than ever. The flow of technology from the free world to the planned economies should teach us a lesson about which system encourages the fruits of innovation and invention.

There is probably not a soul in Europe today who hasn't been reminded that this year marks the bicentennial of the United States. I am fascinated by another bicentennial celebrated this year — that of the publication of Adam Smith's classic treatise on free enterprise, *The Wealth of Nations.* We can certainly benefit from some of the ideas that remain valid because they have passed the test of time.

However, we cannot ignore that the value system which we have adopted is, in many respects, light years away from that of Adam Smith's era. The pace of change of these values seems to speed up every year. I think we are rightfully being challenged to re-examine the way we do business in order to accommodate these new values.

I think this new attitude is due in part to better education today — more people are being educated, and our system of education may be better. The fantastic development of communications media has also been partly responsible for a new questioning attitude. In a way, I can't help but feel that this healthy criticism and questioning — and the better education and access to information — show that our system is working the way it should.

These new attitudes pose challenges for business. Younger people entering business today reject dogmatic, authoritarian management. They wish to be respected as individuals. They perceive a real need for self-fulfillment and satisfaction. This means that business today must offer more than a salary to attract individuals. Work has to be satisfying. And, quite often, we perceive a wish to participate in the decision-making process and share in the results. I think this presents business with a marvellous opportunity to create just the sort of 'community' that will be a living evolving organism. It will be more than the sum of its parts and will benefit each of them because it will be an enterprise in which individuals understand their stake in its success and feel responsible to contribute toward its future. Indeed, if we really believe in democracy, a system in which the citizen has a voice in the affairs of state, then we should accept that in the small community of the enterprise, the employees have the right to a voice in its affairs. This is nothing more than applying the Jeffersonian political concept of creating a community through the identification of individual self-interest with community welfare. This however imposes on individuals the responsibility of being 'good citizens'. Their advice, their positions can be influential only if they accept the goals of the enterprise, if they accept the system.

The key is, of course, to combine the benefits of this new-sought community with the advantages of the current system. This individual voice in the enterprise community can be achieved in several ways. To my mind, there are some crucial principles which should guide the creation of the new community so that we retain what has made it so successful:

1 No organisation can survive anarchy. There must always be a well-defined leadership having the respect of the constituents.

2 Those who have the responsibilities of leadership must not sacrifice the future to short-term benefits.

3 The entrepreneur — and those who bring their capital to the enterprise — have every right to obtain a fair return on their investment and to control what is done with their funds.

4 Management's role should continue to be to make trade-offs between the different constituencies with which the enterprise deals — stockholders, employees, customers and society at large.

5 At the same time, management must be and, in fact is, accountable to each of these groups.

I believe these principles are essential to guarantee the healthy functioning of our system. In view of them, I believe that the best form of participation lies in good employee-manager relationships. This means, on the one hand, a system of planning in which people at many levels are involved. On the other, it implies two-way management communications such that individuals understand and support the objectives of the enterprise, and thus enthusiastically pursue their role in it.

To reach a full participation of employees and an even greater sense of belonging to this community, I believe that a system of stock purchase plans is ideal. I wish it would be adopted by many more companies in Europe as it exists in numerous American companies. Just as I think free enterprise can be even healthier through greater employee interest, I think the system could use a bit of revision in one other sphere: the question of national ownership of firms.

Let me make my position clear. I am not an opponent of

mixed economies, because they can accommodate free enterprise. Nor am I an opponent of nationalised industries in basic public service sectors. My view is that when an industry serves a sole public service nature within a particular domestic market, then it may make sense for the government to run it. I say 'may' make sense because that is not always clear. For example, entrepreneurs in the US say they should be able to compete with the US Post Office because they feel they can do a better job — and considering the fact that there is little difference between regular and express delivery of letters in some US cities, they probably can. While there may be some rationale for public enterprise in some national public services the *rasion d'etre* is entirely lost when you examine the concept of nationalised firms in the international marketplace. That is a confusion of functions, and results prove it. If you look at the record of nationalised firms in competing for international business, it is a bleak one. Consider this: of the top one hundred British exporters in 1975, there were only four nationalised firms. Nationalised firms are so used to being subsidised, protected and untouchable in their own country that they have a hard time competing with private firms on the international market. The more the government gets into the business of business, the bigger the expense for the taxpayer. And that is a vicious cycle. If you look at the nations with the heaviest tax burdens, you see how disincentives to work can actually result from the more onerous tax burdens.

Nationalised industries carry with them other disadvantages. One is the creation of a national monopoly. This, I think, results from an erroneous reading of business imperatives. The key to business success is not the size of the company but the size of the market. As European leaders are now discovering, it would have saved the taxpayer a fortune if there had been three competing European electrical generator companies each constituted by British,

French and German mother companies rather than one big firm in each country. I speak of the real benefits of international competition from the perspective of a business which the *Sunday Times* recently called 'one of the world's most competitive'. Strangely enough, the monopoly effects of nationalisation are recognised by some of nationalised industries' most unyielding proponents. *The Economist* reported that the Rt. Hon. Anthony Wedgwood Benn argued that nationalisation of the British aircraft industry 'will make interlocking decisions in the industry easier to take' and not that it would improve management of the firms. In one important study of your nationalised industries, Professors Graham Reid and Kevin Allen bluntly pointed out that government-owned firms 'often have a considerable degree of monopoly power' and 'are subject to political influence and control' because they are accountable to parliament. This latter point may be the most crucial of all. In a free enterprise system, you have checks and balances where individuals, through their governments, can supervise the proper functioning of enterprises, which are run on neutral economic principles. But in a nationalised industry, you lose this system of checks and balances. You substitute changing political goals for neutral, consistent economic principles. The poor performance of some of these enterprises bears this out. Indeed, I note how public opinion polls here reflect the government's own turn toward encouraging productive private capital investment.

I must say, however, that public understanding of nationalisation leaves much to be desired. Not long ago, I was walking through Harrod's and overheard an American tourist talking to his wife. Surveying the bustling crowds on a day when the Bank of England was straining itself to support the pound, the American turned to his wife and suggested that 'Great Britain ought to nationalise Harrod's to help out the state'.

I do believe that much criticism of the capitalist system is the result of misunderstanding or ignorance of its actual functioning. Recent surveys in the United States for example, show how the role and level of profits in the capitalist system are badly misunderstood. Americans wildly overestimate average corporate profits at thirty-three to forty-five per cent of sales. The real figure is under six per cent. Last spring a public opinion survey was made in France on 'Liberalism versus Collectivism'. A very interesting conclusion was reached. The more people have economic knowledge, the more they are in favor of liberalism or free enterprise if you will. In fact the correlation is just amazing. Unfortunately, I have to say that, in my country — as in many others — economic knowledge is rather at a very low level and that may explain the strong positions of the socialist and communist parties.

In this respect, I was also fascinated by a very recent CBI survey of employees, which showed that there is a great appreciation of the free enterprise system in some unsuspected places. The CBI survey of 1,083 manual workers and 231 managers showed that eighty-six per cent of them felt it was important 'to live in a free enterprise society'. Eighty-two per cent disagreed with the notion that 'profit is a dirty word', accepting the idea that it is a fair way to pay back people for taking the risk of backing an enterprise. This was true even though both workers and managers estimated profits at a minimum twice their real level. Perhaps even more enlightening was the authors' report that many managers had thought that workers did view 'profit' as a dirty word. Some even felt it was best to use a euphemism for it! I think this misunderstanding highlights one place where we have gone wrong. We may be catering to the loudest voices instead of to the majority. We may be addressing ourselves to fashionable arguments without really discovering their importance. We may be wrongly apologising for a system that would appear to need no apologists.

It comes down, I think, to a matter of confidence in

ourselves, as individuals, to be honest with ourselves. We
ought not to be afraid to acknowledge achievements of a
system even if it needs reforms to accommodate new values.
And we ought not to refrain from speaking out in favour of
the profit mechanism at the base of the free enterprise
system, which has served us so well. Indeed, when OECD
finance ministers met in Paris recently they felt it necessary
to emphasise the crucial role of profits in permitting
industry to invest to create new jobs and remove
inflationary supply bottlenecks. I don't think I could put it
more precisely than did Prime Minister Callaghan, on
another occassion, 'if there are no profits, there will be no
jobs'.

It usually surprises people to hear that Sweden, which is
often cited as the model of the 'welfare state', welcomed
free enterprise as the generator of its many and varied social
benefits. Ninety-five per cent of Swedish industry is
privately owned, and reinvestment in new plant and jobs
has been encouraged through tax laws. The Swedes realised
that the only way to generate benefits without enervating
the economy was through continued private investment
and growth. Some commentators on the recent Swedish
elections say that in part, the Swedes voted to keep this free
enterprise system through support for parties that opposed
a plan for a union takeover of some companies. I am
especially intrigued by the analysis of the recent Swedish
elections. It appears that voters concluded that taxes had
reached intolerable levels. They also disapproved of the
encroachments of a growing government bureaucracy.

The bureaucracy is a layer that can stifle business
competition as it can short-circuit the democratic process
through which the individual can be heard by his
government representatives. As I mentioned earlier, it also
has to be fought in the enterprise if individuals are to feel
part of a human organisation and part of a community in
which their initiative is encouraged. In France, a business

recruiting its first apprentice worker needs fourteen copies of five different forms, fifty-five signatures of approval and twenty-two other covering documents. The dangers of bureaucracy and regulation are being recognised in the US. The US Federal Trade Commissioner favours replacing regulation with free competition in several sectors where regulation has actually stifled competition. He cites the startling example of the Florida Construction Licensing Board which, in one recent year, received 2,150 applications from would-be entrepreneurs and rejected every one.

It seems that we have let our good intentions go awry. We have let theory go unchallenged because it was new and exciting and promised ideal results that could not be delivered. This is why we must get back to basics. We must reaffirm that it is improving the material and spiritual lot of the individual that is the base of our endeavours. To my mind, as I have outlined it today, this means realising that the relationship between the individual, the enterprise and the state turns on the relationship between the individual and the enterprise. I noted how through communication and education we must try to create a commonality of interest so that out of the mass of individuals, we create a community. My final point was that our belief in the primacy of the individual can be best backed up through the proper functioning of the free enterprise system, which gives the individual the opportunity to improve his own lot and to determine the products and services he values. If there is a common thread in my talk, it is a challenge to business to regain the trust of individuals, of society, by reinforcing the virtues of this free enterprise system and correcting any abuses of it. For it is only through this trust that a true community can be created out of the individual, the enterprise and the state.

6 The conversion of equity capital and its consequences

Mr. David Harris

Having qualified as a Chartered Accountant David Harris had industrial experience with ITT and Ransome, Hoffman & Pollard before joining Carreras Rothmans as Group Management Accountant. He was Chairman of the company's Working Party on Employee Participation which focused his attention on the ideas in this paper. He continues to be much concerned with the development of employee participation in the company.

The position of Britain in the World in 1976 is so low in the table of nations that Alexander Solzhenitzyn could state recently that Britain was of less significance that 'Uganda or even Rumania' without the comment being generally derided. From a position of great power, wealth and influence we have declined dramatically in the era since the end of the Second World War to the ranks of third class nations. Furthermore, the decline is complete in its character in that we have not traded our military or economic might for a situation in which our people are better fed, educated and housed than could otherwise have been expected.

Some of the more obvious ways in which the deteriorating position of the nation manifests itself are:

- Despite an unrivalled amount of external analysis and introspection, our economy has consistently performed below the levels of competitor nations.

- British social services, which have been a source of considerable pride, are now in many respects inferior to those provided by other developed nations.

- To slow the rate of deterioration in our living standards we have both borrowed heavily and cheapened our currency.

- Our world political influence and moral leadership have declined at least as much as our economy and military power.

- Parliament is much reduced, largely because no government in recent times has commanded a genuine mandate from a sufficient proportion of the population to make its policies generally acceptable. If democracy means 'government by the people' (O.E.D.) our nation is no longer democratic.

Sadly this list is by no means exhaustive, but is sufficient to indicate the magnitude of our difficulties and the critical need for effective action. Unfortunately the way we have approached our national problems in recent years is reminiscent of Oliver Hardy's frequent, exasperated cry to Stan Laurel 'This is a fine mess you've got us into Stanley'. That is to say, it is always someone else's fault, as evidenced by the following reasons produced frequently for our decline:

- We have had too much/too little socialism.

- We have spent too much/too little on public services.

- We have 'gone for growth' when we shouldn't/we have been too cautious and let our opportunities slip.

- The British working man is too lazy/the capitalists have failed to make the investments to provide our workers 'with sufficient power at their elbows'.

- Government has insufficient control over our productive resources/efficient economic management is impossible because of governmental interference and vacillation.

In addition to the above examples, reference is frequently made to historic reasons for our economic failures, such as the outdated structure and attitudes of British trade unions/management and the age and condition of our factories and equipment.

Unfortunately there is sufficient merit in all of the above points, even where they are contradictory, to give a degree of credence which allows the truth to be obscured and our attention directed to consequences not causes.

Furthermore, we should not be surprised by our decline, or its nature. In 1939 Peter Drucker, having fled from Nazi

Germany to England, wrote a book entitled *The End of Economic Man* in which he said: 'Communism and Fascism are doomed to perish from the earth for they are both systems of government that crush human liberty in the interest of the state and deny mens' need for freedom and equality ... capitalism and state socialism are also doomed. The former because mass production is incompatible with human liberty and the latter because it creates a new tyranny in its growing bureaucracy.' Prophetic words indeed when applied to the world's first industrial nation.

Must we assume therefore that our problems are so deep and varied that we are inevitably going to be overwhelmed by them and forced into a totalitarian regime of one hue or another? I cannot accept this proposition because I do not believe that the problems confronting us are necessarily greatese faced by our competitors. For instance, Japan depends even more heavily on imported raw materials than the UK. Furthermore, history shows us time and again that the greatness and prosperity of a nation arise primarily from the will and attitudes of the people, rather than abundance of natural resource. I am led therefore to the conviction that our difficulties lie not in the unique nature of our problems, but in our inability to agree on the solutions. We must therefore ask ourselves, why and how are we different in this respect, and what can be done about it?

It is unfortunately true that more than any other developed country (with the possible exception of Italy), our society is strongly divided. As a consequence, effective leadership, which is fundamental to the success or otherwise of a nation, becomes almost impossible in a democracy. The divisions have been magnified because, in the post war era, the two-party system in Britain has operated in such a way that the apparent choice has been between those advocating socialism and those advocating capitalism — although these terms have in reality largely lost any meaning in this context. In power and in opposition the Conservative and Labour parties have spent the greater part of their energies in negating each others' efforts.

The consequences of such divisions on the inherent stability of society were clearly stated by Adam Smith in *The Theory of Moral Sentiments* published in 1759:
'Society may subsist among different men as among different merchants from a sense of its utility without any mutual love or affection ... society cannot however subsist among those who are at all times ready to hurt and injure one another. The moment that mutual resentment and animosity take place all the bonds of it are broken asunder and the different members of it are, as it were, dissipated and scattered abroad by the violence and opposition of their discordent affections .... *justice is the main pillar that upholds the whole.*'

Unfortunately, in the UK in 1975, whilst the divisions reflect in almost every part of our national life, they operate most strongly in industry to the extent that the use of the strike as a political or economic weapon has become known as 'the English disease'.

I firmly believe that this polarisation of society is against the wishes of the vast majority of the people and based on a misunderstanding of the real nature of our economic society. Fortunately, there is no doubt that our problems can be alleviated if we create a society in which there is a broad consensus on the road ahead for our nation, and a means of electing governments which will ensure that decisions are taken and promoted in line with the consensus view. This situation will partially be achieved by electoral law reform, which gains increasing prominence as our current system becomes even less satisfactory. (The present Labour Government was elected in 1974 by thirty-nine per cent of those voting and twenty-nine per cent of the electorate. How can it therefore claim to have a mandate for any of its policies, let alone those known to be politically

politically unpopular?) However, electoral reform alone will not suffice — to unite the people it must be seen that we are moving to a better, fairer society. To achieve this we must examine the real nature of our society and economic system.

The so-called socialist economies have shown themselves to be very inferior in terms of their ability to produce wealth if compared to the so-called capitalist economies. That they produce societies which are more 'equal' or more 'just' is an arguing point for academics and bigots and one which, as I intend to demonstrate, we need not pursue here. Furthermore, I refer to both economies as 'so-called' because they possess far more in common than their respective theories allow.

Given that this is so, we need a society which is both just and capitalist. We know what is generally meant by 'just' although judgement is required to determine if it applies to any particular case. However, by capitalist I mean a society in which it is recognised that:

- Capital is a resource, like any other resource, that should command a fair or market price

- Capital is a finite resource that must be used wisely if it is to help create wealth

- Capital wisely used, grows, whilst capital badly used, can be consumed and lost forever

- Capital, like income, must be seen to be fairly shared

There is, I believe, little dispute over the first three items. It is in the solution to the last point that the opportunity to resolve our problems lies. If we can create a society in which capital as well as income can be earned and shared with a high degree of social justice (as has generally been the case for income in developed cn recent years), the nature of our society will change. Instead of the divisiveness and revolutionary tendencies of recent years, we will revert to an evolutionary society which will allow genuine progress – particularly for the less fortunate.

George Copeman, in his booklet *Employee Participation in Capital Growth* published by MCB (Management Decision) Limited in 1976 states:

> 'Only 3.8 per cent of those eligible to vote in Britain have a direct shareholding in British industry. Britain's capital owners are so few that they are continually at risk of 'source punishment'. The Law of Social Punishment says: 'Small-minority groups are at risk of social punishment regardless of whether they appear to be privileged or underprivileged'. History contains many examples of both privileged and underprivileged minorities being victimised.
>
> The vendetta against capital in Britain is harmful to the whole economy and it promotes the continuation of an out-of-date ideological battle between the supporters of Adam Smith and those of Karl Marx. Yet neither Smith's description of how capital is accumulated nor Marx's description is an acceptable explanation of how capital is accumulated today inside the successful joint stock company. An up-to-date description of how capital is accumulated leads logically on to a policy of employee participation in capital growth. Britain needs such a policy, as effected in the United States and France, to create shareholders out of employees in the more successful companies and thereby promote a greater sense of employee participation in the economic system.'

Whilst agreeing with his description of the problem, I propose a very different solution.

For most people in Britain, capital, if they have it at all, is
represented by the excess value of their house over the
related mortgage plus the value of their car, household
durables etc., and the capital value of the right to future
pensions. In these terms they would not regard themselves
as capitalists. Who then are the capitalists? Apart from the
small number of persons (hotly pursued by the Revenue
and diminishing steadily) who still have substantial personal
wealth in the UK most of the capital invested in British
industry is held by government, banks, pension funds,
investment trusts, building societies etc. It may therefore be
argued that through these media virtually all citizens are
capitalists. In practical terms however, this contention is not
borne out by the extensive research carried out in this area,
which shows that this 'once removed' relationship has little
meaning. We are therefore left with the image rather than
the substance of the capitalist as the rich and powerful
individual who, by the way he invests or withdraws his
funds, governs the lives of working men and unfairly
benefits from their labours. If, however, it is still possible
effectively to divide our society on the strength of the image
rather than the reality, clearly there is something wrong.

The 'normal' solution (as advocated by George Copeman)
is to encourage companies to participate in some scheme
for issuing shares to employees, thus making them owners
too. Whilst this policy has had some success in France and
America, experience in the U.K. has not been encouraging.
I believe that our circumstances and background are
fundamentally different and a more radical approach is
essential. My solution is as follows:

1   For the purpose of the initial experiment, the
    proposal is limited to companies employing 2,000
    people or more. This has been found to be a
    convenient measure abroad for two-tier board
    systems.

2   All ordinary capital in such companies i.e. capital entitling the owners to residual profits whether distributed or retained to be converted to fixed interest capital at a rate based on the open market value (probably averaged over a suitable period to ensure fairness).

3   The annual general meeting of the company to be made up of employee and loan stock capital representatives in agreed proportions. (This could be done on various European models whether or not there is an unitary or two-tier board system).

4   If fresh capital is required, the company competes in the existing, established market with government, local government, banks, building societies etc. The rate to be paid will depend on the standing and prospects of the company.

5   The consequences of this simple proposal are radical and powerful:

    –   the cost of capital will be charged fully against profits like any other basic resource (raw materials, labour, cost of accommodation etc.).

    –   after charging all costs and taxes (if any), any remainder is available for two purposes only — re-investment in the business and/or additional payment to the employees. (Ideally this would be by way of fixed interest loan stock but it could be a simple bonus.)

    –   If there are losses, the holders of loan stock will continue to receive the full payment for the capital they provide, if and until the company goes out of business. This is not so with ordinary dividends.

    –   The whole relationship between the employee and

the enterprise will have changed fundamentally and must have powerful repercussions on such matters as:

industrial relations
wage negotiations
responsibility and response

There are a number of obvious questions that this proposal raises, and I deal with them below:

1 Is this proposal technically feasible?

(a) I attach as an appendix a random sample of twenty leading UK companies which shows:

- the book value of the ordinary shareholders funds according to their 1975 accounts
- the 1975 market values (high and low) of the ordinary share capital
- the average percentage returns on all three values
- in all cases, the book value exceeds the 1975 market low, and with three exceptions also exceeds the 1975 unweighted average

(b) To obtain a conversion which will provide the equity shareholder with a fair price for his shares, I propose that:

- The market value be averaged over a suitable period.
- The book value of equity shareholders funds is to be issued as fully paid loan stock at an interest rate based on the standing of the company and previous years returns.
- Where the book value so issued exceeds the market value, the shareholders are receiving the value their ownership entitles them to, based on net asset book

values. That this differs from the market rating is more likely to be due to market volatility than book-keeping methods.

- Where the book value is lower than the market value, this means that the market has taken a bullish attitude to the company which is probably based on anticipation of high future revenues or the possibility of realising a capital gain. To compensate the shareholders for at least the partial loss of anticipated future gains, they should be entitled to an amount of additional fixed loan stock to be paid for out of future profits (at a rate to be agreed with employee representatives).

- The methods outlined above are not the only ways in which the conversion could be achieved with a considerable degree of fairness. Various other options are open, including the ways in which nationalised industries have acquired ownership. They do however, demonstrate that the concept is a practical one.

2 Is it acceptable from the viewpoint of the ordinary shareholder?

In my view, very much so, because:

(a) He receives a fair value for his shares.

(b) He is likely to obtain a higher rate of return with much greater security.

(c) He retains an interest in the assets of the company, and any capital growth.

(d) From the appendix, it can be seen that the return on shareholders funds was unacceptably low. Furthermore, if these funds were inflation adjusted, the return would diminish much further, i.e. the

Company	Capital values			
	Ordinary shares at par value	Ordinary shareholders funds	1975 Market Value	
			High	Low
	£000's	£000's	£000's	£000's
Allied Breweries Ltd.	120,715	299,191	366,974	164,172
Bass Charrington	69,449	336,749	305,576	125,008
Booker McConnell	13,749	46,066	50,596	15,674
BAT	65,460	1,003,250	233,038	106,045
Cadbury Schweppes	91,260	166,724	210,726	73,296
Danish Bacon Co.	3,312	7,322	4,902	1,987
Debenhams	19,986	97,833	71,950	19,187
Fitch Lovell	9,695	32,833	35,144	12,604
Gallaher	42,528	154,617	137,791	136,090
Great Universal Stores	62,150	337,574	560,593	215,039
A. Guinness	21,275	109,086	121,693	47,656
House of Fraser	30,377	137,213	116,648	43,743
Imperial Group	176,484	706,263	589,457	222,370
J. Lyons	30,896	135,767	52,157	16,974
Marks & Spencer	162,251	345,824	843,705	298,541
Tesco	15,626	68,771	167,198	67,191
Trust House Forte	20,918	90,874	107,100	32,631
Unilever	45,867	580,367	796,251	307,309
Whitbread	56,222	248,206	170,915	76,461
F.W. Woolworth	94,537	193,814	276,048	94,531
Average	57,638	254,917	260,923	103,820

		Percentage returns on		
Shares at par value	Ordinary shareholders funds	1975 market value		
		High	Low	Medium
%	%	%	%	%
19.7	7.9	6.5	14.5	10.5
24.1	5.0	5.5	13.4	9.5
16.4	4.9	4.5	14.4	9.5
67.6	4.4	19.0	41.7	30.3
11.1	6.1	4.8	13.9	9.4
11.4	4.7	7.0	17.3	12.1
24.7	5.0	6.8	25.7	16.2
23.0	6.8	6.4	17.7	12.0
31.5	8.7	9.7	9.9	9.8
37.2	6.9	4.1	10.8	7.4
35.2	6.9	6.1	15.7	10.9
23.9	5.3	6.2	16.6	11.4
28.4	7.1	8.5	22.5	15.5
11.3	2.6	6.7	20.5	13.6
19.7	9.2	3.8	10.7	7.2
37.1	8.4	3.5	8.6	6.0
45.2	10.4	8.8	29.0	18.9
72.5	5.7	4.2	10.8	7.5
17.9	4.1	5.9	13.2	9.5
24.3	11.9	8.3	24.3	16.3
28.0	6.3	6.2	15.6	10.9

companies are not paying a fair rate for the capital
they consume!

3 Is the proposal likely to be acceptable to employees in times of low profitability or loss?

(a)   Whilst the employees would not be entitled to
      income beyond their emoluments in these
      circumstances, they would not be in a worse
      position than presently. Furthermore, they would
      have much greater incentive to play their part in
      ensuring that the company does not find itself in this
      situation.

(b)   In the case of an industry or company which is
      basically not viable, this proposal will neither help
      nor hinder individual enterprises. The employees
      are, however, very likely to be either pressing hard
      for improvements or leaving for companies which
      offer prospects of income and capital growth. We
      have seen clearly that policies of unrealistically
      maintaining jobs by overmanning or propping up
      unviable companies is costly and damaging.

(c)   In a growing, prosperous economy (which this
      proposal would help generate) further jobs would
      arise in wealth creating companies offering good
      employment.

4 What is the affect on the supply of genuine risk capital?

This question is fundamental to our prospects of creating
wealth from new sources. Because the proposal is limited to
companies employing over 2,000 persons:

(a) The amount of risk capital available to meet the needs of smaller companies or persons with new ideas or machines etc., will be enhanced.

(b) Major established companies raise capital for new ventures usually from internal cash flows or their bankers.

(c) If a small enterprise succeeds to the point that it employs more than 2,000 people, it will then convert. The lucky shareholders may then chose to hold their loan stock or realise it and invest in a new risk venture.

In addition to the questions answered above, I believe a number of points should be made:

- When companies were badly squeezed by inflation recently, the additional funds to keep them alive did not come from the equity market, but were provided by the banks and institutions — fixed interest lenders.

- Anything which increases the general level of prosperity, encourages positive attitudes to wealth creation and helps eliminate doctrinaire class distinctions must be for the good of all.

- In my view, speculation in the shares of the companies which form our major national wealth creating asset, is not acceptable in a responsible society.

Conclusion

It is my belief that given political goodwill this proposal contains no overwhelming practical problems, and the general benefits it would convey are immense. By avoiding the trap that the only alternative to our present society is more socialism with its attendant, inevitable decline in living standards and personal freedom we can:

- create a society where personal wealth is a genuine possibility for all
- by sensible use of the taxation mechanism, ensure that there is not unacceptable disparity between highest paid and lowest paid and rich and poor
- re-generate our national wealth to enable us to provide a level of service in health, education, overseas aid etc. of which we can again be proud.
- begin to eliminate the class attitudes which have been so destructive in the past.

7   Towards worker ownership

Sir Bernard Miller

Sir Bernard was for twelve years Chairman of the John Lewis Partnership, and with this long experience of managing in a large organisation without equity shareholders, he was invited to contribute a short critique of the Harris proposals in the previous chapter.

I believe very firmly that equity capital should be abolished but I reach that conclusion by a different route from Mr. Harris and I differ from him in my assessment of the significance of its abolition for the achievement of a fundamental change in the present industrial climate.

I have a vested interest in this topic. I am still a partner in the John Lewis Partnership — an organisation which has no equity capital, yet has accumulated £130 million of capital reserves and now has a turnover of some £350 million a year. So it is not surprising that I support Mr. Harris, although by a different route.

Mr. Harris, in my view, rightly identifies equity capital as responsible for an image of capitalism which, although largely false, has a divisive effect on our social and industrial structure, which in turn is largely responsible for our lamentable industrial performance. That image is epitomised in the public joint stock company.

Under company law, a company must be operated primarily for the benefit of its shareholders, who alone are members of the company. Control of the company rests with the equity shareholders, who are entitled in perpetuity to the residual profits of the business. At the same time, it was the principle of limited liability that made possible the tremendous growth of joint stock companies, so that equity shareholders demand unlimited profits but limit their own liability for losses. How anybody can justify this really defeats me. To my mind it is totally unjustifiable; a view I reach more by emotion than pragmatic analysis.

In my view, there was never any justification for the equity principle in respect of shareholders who were not themselves entrepreneurs. All risks are measurable and high risks in lending money to others require high but not unlimited rewards. It is from equity shareholding that many of the evils of the so-called capitalist system stem — capital profits, company manipulation, financial speculation, insider trading, etc. Its inherent wrongness has been implicitly acknowledged in the continuing attempt by governments of both political parties to limit dividends and tax capital gains and to counter the manifold evasions of taxation to which that gives rise.

Instead of trying to mitigate the consequences of the evil, it is better to remove the evil altogether, along the lines suggested by Mr. Harris, or other similar ways. Equity capital is, in reality, becoming a hollow concept in most large companies, where profits are increasingly determined by factors outside the influence or control of the owners of the capital: government regulations and trade union power are in many cases the major factors in determining what share of the earnings of the business shall go to shareholders.

It will be said that to abolish equity capital will produce a flight of capital abroad and that industry will be hamstrung from loss of investment capital. This need not be so. The experience of the past twenty years shows that the government can effectively control the movement of capital and present thinking points to increasing government involvement in the field of capital investment. There is no evidence that the wide range of constraints upon capital, dividend limitation, wealth taxation, exchange controls, etc. has led to any significant exodus of capital or prevented the formation of new capital. Moreover, the contribution of private equity capital to the total of new investment is now minimal. CSO statistics showed that the amount of equity capital raised for industrial and commercial companies in the five years to the end of 1974 averaged £124m per annum compared with £3059m from undistributed income and £2752m from bank finance: in that period equity capital provided only six per cent of fixed capital formation.

For all these reasons, I believe that the abolition of equity capital is both feasible and necessary for any significant improvement in industrial relations but I do not believe that either by itself, or accompanied by the change in company law envisaged by Mr. Harris, especially with reference to the Bullock Report, will suffice. Replacing control by equity shareholders with control by loan stockholders will still leave the basic conflict relationship between unions and employers and the effect of the Bullock Report would merely extend the conflict into the Boardroom. I see no reason why loan stockholders who replace equity shareholders should have any greater power in the control of companies than do existing loan stockholders — in Mr. Harris's own words 'Capital is a resource, like any other resource, that should command a fair or market price' but no more. If equity capital disappears, the reality of ownership and control must rest with the total body of workers, management and managed alike, and there would be some trust deed of partnership between them, prescribing the principles and procedures upon which the business shall operate. Unless the removal of equity capital reduces the whole role of capital to a resource to be hired like any other and no more, the psychological effect of removing it will be small. I believe that we can only get a new spirit in industry by the fundamental shift to worker ownership of the business, with a structure which provides for proper management authority, subject to complete accountability. I regard the removal of equity capital and reform of company law as a clearing away of dead wood to make possible fresh constructive development. But I do believe that there is a strong psychological barrier to the improvement of relationships in this country — and that we ought to make the effort.

8 A certain sort of freedom

Graham Turner

Graham Turner is now a freelance author and journalist having been Economics Correspondent of the BBC. He is a regular contributor to The Sunday Telegraph. His publications include 'The Leyland Papers', 'The Car Makers', 'The Persuasian Industry' and 'Business in Britain'. He was awarded the John Player Award for Management Journalism in 1972 and presented the paper 'A New Philosophy for Industry and Society'.

He has been a Visiting Fellow of the Oxford Management Centre for some years.

I am not usually a great one for semantics, but on this occasion I want to spend a little time looking at the title given to this series of lectures, because it seems to me to enshrine implications which are entirely misleading.

To begin with, by putting the enterprise between the individual and the state, it suggests — or so it seems to me — that companies act as buffers between the liberty-loving individual and the liberty-limiting state; and this suggestion is reinforced by the use of the word 'enterprise' which, in the lingering mythology of capitalism, conjures up images of bold, swash-buckling entrepreneurs, latter-day Drakes, no-nonsense individualists beholden to no man (let alone governments) characters who would defend the individual and his liberty to the last drop of blood. The enterprise, both the juxtaposition and the word imply, is a haven of liberty, a bulwark of individual freedom.

Nothing, I believe, could be further from the reality. I can think of few bodies *less* concerned with the individual and his freedom than big corporations — if it is not big trade unions. Of course, the men who beat the drums of corporate virtue would have us believe it is far otherwise: none more so, it would seem, than those who labour for multi-nationals which operate near-monopolies in many countries, turn out products which can be used to endanger individual privacy and freedom and are often somewhat conformist in their corporate style. You have to admire the sheer, downright cheek of a man who can issue forth from such an environment and talk about individual freedom.

Just look at the record. Which of us, I wonder, can name six big companies which have backed the rights of the individual when the economic interests of the corporation were at stake. Or just one which has stood firm in defending, say, an individual's right not to belong to a trade union on the ground of conscience. The NUR, it seems, doth make cowards of us all. 'Well, of course, the principle is good', our free-speaking liberty-loving, truth-at-any-price Public Relations Director will tell inquirers, 'and, of course, we all support the idea, but you know how it is …. and when you get down to it (and that is what I do all the time), that fellow is definitely a bit of an odd-ball. Doesn't get on at all well with his mates, you know. And the jobs of thousands of other people (mine included, of course) depend on us finding a formula to keep the unions happy …. And then, don't forget, we have got the new product coming out next month and, in these circumstances we really cannot afford to be disrupted by a little local difficulty of this kind. Mind you, we shall see he's well looked after — as a matter of fact we've got a pretty good idea where he could get another job'.

Then take the case of the foreman who reprimanded someone for shoddy work, or perhaps even went as far as going onto the assembly line without asking for the shop steward's permission. Do the goodly fellowship of superintendents and the noble army of middle managers praise him? And what about the glorious company of senior managers, do they acknowledge and magnify him? They do not. Never have you heard such a coughing and a wheezing, such a shuffling and a cringing. 'Yes, yes, it is quite true — he was only doing his job and, as a matter of fact, he was quite right — but I really do wish he would keep his nose out of trouble. I'm afraid the only thing we can do now is find a formula to get him off the hook. Find some way of moving him without hurting his dignity.' And God help the manager who cannot come up with a good formula!

At a higher level, it is much the same. 'Freedom of speech?' — we are right at the top now, having lunch with the liberty-loving chairman. 'Why, yes indeed, we would not be where we are today as a company if all we had was yes-men, now would we? What we need are people who speak their minds, independent-minded chaps who will stand up and be counted.' Like, for example, a friend of mine who was recently offered a job by the BBC. He felt he ought to tell them he had got a book on television coming out — not outrageously critical but suggesting, among other things, what the future shape of television ought to look like. Not long after he had let them see the manuscript, he had a little phone-call just to say — in the nicest possible way, of course — that they were afraid it would not quite do, that they hoped he would still feel able to join them, but …. my friend, to his infinite credit, told the BBC what they could do with their job. Like Ron Lucas, Finance Director of BMC, who made the mistake of telling Leyland the truth about his company's figures slap, bang in the middle of the merger talks — and after the BMC chairman had said something quite different too. And like John Barber, selected for the part of sacrificial goat by the Ryder committee as part of their plan, whose effect, I believe, will be to fund the dissolution of British Leyland. Now, everybody knew that there were others on the British Leyland Board who were just as responsible for the company's situation as John Barber — and who might, on a reasonable view of what the word conscience implies, have elected either to go with him, or at least to speak for him. Did anyone have the guts to resign with him? Or to speak a word in his defence? I am afraid not. From where I was standing, the silence was deafening. Not a cheep from all those independent-minded chaps standing up and being counted. Well, they may have said to themselves, perhaps it is all for the best in the long-term interests of the Corporation, perhaps it is necessary that one man should die for the people of Longbridge and Cowley and Berkeley Square House. And the rights of the individual? Well, perhaps we had better leave the lawyers to sort them out. Indeed, far from being concerned with the individual and his freedom in a negative, protective sense, many big corporations act in a way which seems intended positively to destroy the individuality of their executives. I have always thought, for example, that the steady and persistent brainwashing to which corporate executives are subjected is quite as thorough as that undergone by any Marxist. Attitudes, dress, nothing is left out. Perhaps it is only Japanese companies who sing hymns, but most of the others have their approved texts.

The fact is that, much as many big corporation executives may dislike the thought, they are far more like big trade unions than they would care to acknowledge. You sometimes hear them discoursing in a superior way about trade unionists who have sent one of their mates to Coventry. But what, I wonder, happens when it gets about that so-and-so has been put in the dog-house by the m.d. for pulling a colossal boo-boo? What would they call the silence which then surrounds so-and-so like a cloud? Sending him to Leamington Spa, I suppose. And those terrible kangaroo courts which those uncivilised total-itarians in the unions hold from time to time — what about them? Well, are the principles behind them very different from the coups and the purges which remove unwanted executives from their seats — with the minimum of fuss and embarrassment, of course? One man, only one man, you know .. and I expect he will soon get over it. Some of them even go to the funeral — just to show loyalty, I suppose.

The fact is, of course, that both corporations and trade unions are, in essence, collectives; and in both of them, solidarity is the name of the game.

But, you may be saying to yourself, all this is entirely natural — and I would agree. I am not for a moment suggesting that the kind of attitudes and behavior I have been describing are anything abnormal or untoward, simply illustrating my point that the individual, and his several freedoms, have no part in the essential purposes of corporations. Corporations are groupings of people and resources for the purpose of economic self-interest, and when the interests of the individual militate against the corporation's economic self-interest, then the individual has to yield.

So, sadly, we must say farewell to those passionate individualists which the word 'enterprise' conjures up; and, reluctantly, accept that 'corporation' is simply the capitalist way of describing its form of collective.

But, you may say, are you not just talking about the IBMs and the ICIs and the British Leylands — and is it not rather different in small companies? Is it not there that the pure milk of individualism can best be found? There may, I agree, be differences, but nothing like as great as the mythology suggests. A small company provides an opportunity for a man or a relatively small group of men (or women) to exercise their commercial talents with greater freedom and, while the company remains in their control, provides them with a certain security against the danger of being taken over. Now that kind of environment may encourage individual virtues like courage and outspokenness to flourish, but not necessarily. I could name you one or two family-owned businesses which are more tyrannical in their operations than, say, ICI. Solidarity, and a feudal sort of solidarity at that, is still the order of the day; and the individual is as free as a bird so long as he has the right surname. Please do not think I am against small companies — enterprises you could even call them — because for me they exemplify one of the great strengths of capitalism; but I think it is worth making the point that they are created to fulfil the economic self-interest of a man or a small group of men and not to act as bulwarks of individual liberty. Whether they do that or not depends entirely on the individuals at the top.

But, I can well see, it might be argued that, even so, the corporation — though perhaps unconsciously and indirectly — aids the individual by providing him with a haven from the encroaching power of the state simply by existing as a separate and distinct empire of its own. I think that, if you want to use that argument, you have —as you go — to answer the question as to whether a senior civil servant has greater or less scope for individual freedom than a senior executive of, say British Rail; and, at the end of the day, you have to face up to the increasing inter-dependence of the state and the big corporations, private as well as public. Just look at a few of the more obvious facts and figures. Sixty per cent of all spending in this country is undertaken by Government, central and local (the comparable figure for Chile at the time Allende took over was, incidentally, forty per cent); and, as and if that figure rises, there will presumably be fewer and fewer corporate bosses willing to say ''boo' to the Whitehall goose. That is not to mention the fact that government can, and does, control the prices a corporation may charge, the salaries it pays to its managers, where it may build its factories and who it can take over; or the fact that, in the day of trouble, *pace* British Leyland, Harland and Wolff and all the rest of that heavenly host, it is Whitehall and its minions who have to act as ultimate saviour. So what we have here are two increasingly inter-locking economic interests; a partner-ship, utterly natural, between giants whose interests — stability, certainty and so on — overlap in so many essentials.

I was much intrigued by what I found on two visits to Sweden this year, one before the recent General Election, one after. On the first visit, I was appalled by what I saw, a good example of what I call the Corpulent State, and with individual outspokenness not greatly in evidence. I can best illustrate the impact it made on me by telling one or two stories. One day, the producer and I were having lunch with five young Swedish radicals, teachers in a retraining college, and one of them, a nice girl, said she had been to Northern Ireland. The producer asked her who she had talked to there. 'A lot of Catholics,' she replied 'but no Protestants.'

And what had she done when she got back? Started a fund
for political prisoners. At this point, the producer —
knowing that funds for political prisoners have a habit of
ending up as metal pellets in people's backs — saw blue.
'Yes,' he said, leaning forward, 'and we're going to start a
fund for political prisoners in Sweden'. 'How interesting',
said the girl, 'which ones?' 'All eight million of you', he
replied, with some venom. The really interesting thing,
though, was that not one of these five reacted in any way —
apart from a slight flush on the gills of one or two of them.
It was the same sort of thing over a dinner table. The
subject of Solzhenitsyn came up and I said I thought he was
a great man. 'But is he not anti-Communist?' asked one of
the young men at the table. 'I should hope so,' I replied.
After all, if you have seen 100 million people slaughtered in
your lifetime, it must be pretty hard to be for the regime
that did it'. 'Now', said the host tactfully, 'I think it is time
to have a cup of coffee in another room'.

It was just as hard to get people to speak their minds. We
did an interview with a friend of Ingmar Bergman, of 105
per cent tax fame — and the friend is an outstanding film
director and playwright. At last, I thought, here is
somebody who will be really outspoken. When we arrived,
he took me aside and said apologetically, 'You will
understand how tricky the situation is, so I have typed out
both the questions and the answers. Would you like a
copy?' It was much the same with a don at Stockholm
University, a man who said over coffee in his room that he
worked there because it was one of the few places left in
Sweden where you could still speak your mind. Wonderful,
I thought. But, as we walked outside to the cameras, he
suddenly muttered, half under his breath, 'Now, I must be
positive'. I slowly began to understand why we had been
told that so many of the American Vietnam deserters have
now left Sweden — ironically, because they found they were
losing their aggression.

It was the first Western country I have ever been to where I felt Group-think was really practised, where the individual had somehow begun to disappear in the interests of solidarity, where it was desperately hard to make an individual stand against the unspoken consensus. Those same pressures, of course, exist in this country, and they are increasing, but thus far, not at quite the same intensity as I saw them in Sweden in May. There are people here, for example, who look down on women who devote themselves to bringing up their children — 'just mothers', I believe the phrase is. In Sweden, such misguided, not to say anti-social creatures are labelled *lyxfru* — luxury wives.

It all reminded me very much of Japan, where I remember talking to a young manager at Toyo Kogyo, which as you will know produces Mazda cars in Hiroshima. He told me how he had been very quarrelsome at school and how his teacher used to keep him back for an hour two or three nights a week and talk to him in an effort to make him less quarrelsome. Society, the teacher used to tell him, depends on co-operation. It was the same at home. His parents did not ask him how he had got on with his lessons; what they wanted to know was how he was getting on with his classmates. So I asked him how things were going in the company. Fine, he said, they had discussions but not arguments. But how had he managed to change so much, I asked. Well you know, he said, society depends on co-operation.

I may add that, when it came to giving our programme a title, we ran into the BBC's own, unspoken consensus. I was quite keen on the notion of *Grave New World*. Too political, thought our masters. It finished up as *The Swedish Model*.

So, I was particularly interested to go back to Sweden the other week, to see what effect the departure of the Socialists after forty-four long years had had on the national psyche and, more particularly, on business attitudes. I went, I suppose, expecting to hear a wholehearted emotional sigh of relief — and that, in part, was what I did hear. Businessmen told me jubilantly how delighted they were that the Socialist advance had been checked. The plans for the nationalisation of the banks and the pharmaceutical companies would be scrapped. Committees, largely composed of civil servants, which had been considering whether there might by a central control of product development, to try to eliminate unsuitable items, would almost certainly come to different conclusions than they would have done if the Social Democrats had remained in power. And, above all else, the Meidner plan — to transfer, say twenty per cent of the profits of all the bigger companies into equity shares and then put them into a collectively-owned and controlled employee fund — that was dead, for the time being anyway.

A perfectly comprehensible rapture, I think you will agree. What did surprise me, however, was the way in which the heads of several big companies then separated the personal reactions from their reactions as corporate men. Personally, they said, and in principle, they were all for the new Centre-Right Government but, from the company's point of view, it might have been better in some ways if the Social Democrats had remained in office — much as they hated to say it. When one inqured why, it came down to the fact that the Social Democrats, or at least their Finance Minister, Gunnar Sträng, had been very much on big business's side; that there had been excellent contacts between him and the big corporate bosses; that, when a big company ran into difficulties, it had always been able to do a backstairs deal with Sträng; and that, when the employers ran into wage negotiation difficulties with the unions, they could normally count on Sträng talking quietly to the unions and impressing them with the need for stabilisation. 'We had good contacts and they understood us', one managing director said to me rather plaintively. Others, like one of the big oil companies and a steel business that is going through very deep waters, actually stood to make a cash gain from the return of the Socialists. The oil company, for example, was going to sell off to the state a slice of its under-utilised refinery and was very happy to go along with its plan to set up a state-owned oil business because it felt it might pick up what I believe is called a piece of the action. The new government, the oil company managing director said sadly, was not going any further into the oil business — so he still had all his refinery on his hands. So the retreat, perhaps temporary, of the corporate state was costing his company money — and he was not happy about it. One or two of the senior executives I talked to even went so far as to say that, provided the Socialists were willing to drop the Meidner proposals and to be more moderate than they had become in recent years, why then, perhaps it might be better if Sweden went back to them and had a Social Democrat government again. That was probably the best way of getting on with the trade unions, the best guarantee of holding out the Communists — and so on.

In other words, quite a few of these men, with their *corporate* hats on, would have been quite happy to go on with the system as before, provided only that their control over their empires was not disturbed. They would not have complained about a situation where, to put it mildly, the freedom of the individual and individual expression did not play an outstanding role — provided that they were allowed to get on with their business. In the corporate state, big speaks to big and likes what it hears. And what has the individual got to complain about, with a range of social services which permits him to live in comfort and die in luxury?

So much, though, for Sweden's present, with the light which it sheds for us on the basic rules of the corporate state. What, however, of our own future prospects? In economic and personal terms, a tough and a murky one, I am afraid.

I see unemployment remaining very high, largely because

all I think we are seeing at the moment is a relatively small proportion of the concealed unemployment we have had for a long time in this country coming to the surface. Those who ought to know in Whitehall reckon we have six to seven million too many people in the economy as a whole — and a lot of our enterprises, public and private, are, in one sense, gigantic work-sharing arrangements.

Inflation is going to continue to run at perilously high levels, whichever government is ruling us. The reason is quite simple. The politicians will find the social strains of cutting living standards too much for them except for relatively brief periods and then only by the favour of the trade unions. Inflation is, therefore, apparently the only alternative to social tensions of an unacceptable level in an economy which is often competitive only by virtue of a falling exchange-rate.

More and more sectors of the British economy will become less and less competitive internationally — as the pressures increase and competition gets tougher. For some, including us, 1977 could be a crunch year particularly if the so-called boom continues to peter out.

So where does all that leave us? What, for example, will the trade unions do in such a situation? Well, I believe that, even though the government has signally failed to deliver what men like Jack Jones were hoping for from the Social Contract, they will continue to urge restraint on their members in some form or other — simply because the alternative, a free-for-all, would, as they see it, be even worse. Depending on how long the crisis continues, they may very well be forced to buy some of the nostrums of the Left — if only because nothing else has seemed to work. But essentially, they will be seeking to maintain the stability of the system. Now, that — of course, is an enormous gamble for the trade unions, because what they are doing is no less than risking their own authority with their members, and hence perhaps even their present forms of organisation.

What is more, they may not always ot always have leaders as
charismatic as Jack Jones to hold them together. So they are,
as you might say, at a turning-point in their credibility —
and certainly in their basic function. But, as it seems to me,
at least, they are likely to take the line that their basic
interest — like that of the big corporations and the
government — is in the stability of the system. The Holy
Trinity of the corporate state, in other words, will probably
be at one, for the foreseeable future at least.

The implications of all this are, I think, quite clear. We
are going to see a greater and greater emphasis on the need
for collective action, more and more interference in the
economy by the government, more and more deals
between trade unions, big corporations and government. In
the process, I have no doubt, all of us will be asked to
sacrifice economic and other freedoms. As the ship sinks
lower in the water, we shall be asked to give up something
to help stop it sinking altogether; in other words, to put the
social equilibrium of the country before our individual
choice. We face this prospect, one has to say, without the
deep tradition of collective action, of instinctive solidarity
which is a strong feature of Swedish society and which, in
terms of economic stability, is so powerful an ally. In this
context, I can at least understand all the arguments about
the need to create a more cohesive and less differentiated
society. If what you want is to maintain the stability of a
nation in steep economic decline, then they are persuasive
arguments; and certainly, more persuasive to me than the
sabre-rattling from the prep-school sector of the Tory
Party.

Where, then, does all this leave the individual, who one
might be forgiven for thinking was the point of it all? In a
much less glum situation than you might imagine, and for
two reasons. First, it is adversity and not ease which brings
out the finest qualities and the truest aspirations of the
human spirit; and secondly, because I do not believe that

true individual freedom is determined by external circumstances. I can best illustrate what I mean by pointing to the experience of some of the Russian dissidents in the dungeons of the new Tsarism. I do not know how many of you have read their accounts of the discoveries they have made in those dungeons; but, if you have not, do, because I have seen nothing more heartening for a long time. It is not just Solzhenitsyn; it is also Panine (the Sologdin of Solzhenitsyn's novel *The First Circle*) and Siniavski and Schifrin and others. Again and again, in what they have written, the same message emerges. Incarceration, they say, has been the most important and fruitful experience of their lives because, through it — shorn of all possessions and loved ones — they have discovered what they now consider the real freedom. What is that real freedom? 'How can we', Solzhenitsyn asks, 'free him, who is unfree in his soul?' and Schifrin replies: 'He alone is free, who frees himself from the wretchedness of *inner* slavery'.

What seems to have happened to these men is that, directly confronted as they were with an overwhelming power of evil, they discovered for the first time within themselves an amazing strength, a strength as a Yugoslavian dissident called Mihailov, now serving seven years in prison puts it 'beyond the reach of those outward, seemingly invincible forces'. That strength, he says, is based on the willingness of a man to obey and trust what he calls 'the inner voice of freedom', to walk with that 'mysterious inner power, which in the language of religion is called God'. The essential pre-condition of being able to claim that new strength, he goes on, is 'to renounce everything which the forces of the visible world can take from him'. '. 'Above all', says Solzhenitsyn, 'do not cling to life, free yourself from everything'; Panine adds that 'only he who renounces everything becomes completely free', i.e. that freedom begins where there is nothing more to lose.

Pretty old stuff, you may say, but rather basic. And the

fact that these men discovered the validity of these old truths in circumstances of the worst imaginable oppression gives me great hope. If they can manage it, well then, perhaps the poor, embattled middle manager can make the same discovery — and so can I, even though a good many things which I love may be disappearing from our world. And fortunately, the ability to make that discovery will not be affected by outward circumstances, but by inner attitudes.

Those who spend their lives plotting their own careers; those who make a god of material possessions; those who do not stand in the face of injustice will never find it, whatever the circumstances. That, essentially, is why those who knew him said they never saw Paul Getty really smile.

We are as a nation about to embark on our own Long March. With all our imperial power and much of our economic power gone, we are setting out together to discover what it is that we truly hold in common. It will mean learning to walk together in new ways. If we do not learn quickly enough, we are finished. And at the heart of it all, for the individual, is the great truth of William Penn: 'Men must choose to be governed by God or they condemn themselves to be ruled by tyrants'.

If they are governed by God, the experience of Solzhenitsyn and the others suggests, no tyrant — external or internal — can claim them. If they are not — Mr. Getty's example implies — no amount of prosperity or success can ever save them.

9   The Philosophical scrum

Sir Ian Bancroft

Sir Ian Bancroft has been Permanent Secretary to the Department of the Environment since 1975. After Balliol College and service in the Rifle Brigade he entered the Treasury in 1947; was Private Secretary to Sir Henry Smith, to the Chancellor of the Exchequer and to the Lord Privy Seal. He served in the Cabinet Office and was Principal Private Secretary to successive Chancellors of the Exchequer. He then served as Under-Secretary to the Treasury and Civil Service Department, of which he was subsequently Second Permanent Secretary.

He is also a Visiting Fellow of Nuffield College, Oxford.

The subject of these lectures has occupied the minds of political philosophers since the time of Pericles. The ball is still in play. Despite repeated mauling from the entire philosophical scrum — from Hooker to Locke — the issue remains undecided. Each man must make up his own mind as to the proper role of the individual, the enterprise and the state and about the nature of the relationship between the three.

But even though the question is so difficult, particularly at this moment, we, as a community, cannot afford to drop out. We have to take a view and in fact we do and it may be a different view from the horders of and the dealers in sterling. The importance of this is well illustrated in Professor Robert Dahl's work (*Polyarchy*, Yale University Press) on what makes countries tend towards democracy or totalitarianism. He suggests that two factors are more important than any others in deciding the nature of social and political organisation. Surprisingly, perhaps, these crucial factors are not economic or from my point of view, disappointingly, environmental. They are, in fact, chance and the force of ideas. Perhaps there is little we can do about chance except to recognise it for the potent force it is and to organise ourselves so that we can respond to the unexpected. There is, as we all know, in our private and in our corporate lives the effect of chance. The second factor, the force of ideas, is central to this series of lectures. How we think and what we think is probably far more important than, say, the discovery that there is oil and gas to be had from the North Sea. So what do we think? Clearly, we do not all agree on the form of social, economic and political organisation, but certain political ideas are generally accepted not only in this country but in the EEC and the Western bloc generally. There is the old differentiation between the ideological society and the acquisition society i.e. dynamic society v passive society. One could go on analysing and analysing.

Human rights

These ideas concern human rights. You will remember Beveridge's four freedoms. These were supplemented and elaborated in the Universal Declaration of Human Rights approved by the UN in December 1948. Governments were not acting independently of their citizens in making these declarations. For example, the overwhelming majority of people in this country believe without question in freedom from slavery, due process of law, freedom of association and so on. Certainly one of these beliefs — widely held but politically controversial and difficult to operate in practice — is both the right to work and freedom from exploitation at work. Obviously that belief, and ones like it, are powerful and highly relevant to the subject of this talk. These beliefs influence and shape the relationships established between the individual, the enterprise and the state.

Great expectations

Moreover, the economic development and the technological advances made in Western Europe have given individuals increasingly higher expectations, some might say that in some countries these aspirations are unrealistically high. People believe not only in their right to work, but also in their right to do so in safety and in a satisfying job. And they and their employers are not content to be at the mercy of the trade cycle. They want growth, more wages, higher profits, better standards every year or at least stability. The community's expectations have consistently risen in, a pessimist would say, a secular way, the optimist would say a spectacular way over the last thirty years; and some people maintain that these expectations can be satisfied only by

1)   action by the state, and

2)   acceptance by the enterprise and the individual that
     their relations with each other and with the state
     may need to be — in some cases must be — changed
     if their wants are to be met.

It seems to me, though, that we cannot sensibly talk only
about the individual, the enterprise and the state. This is
because the relationship between the three is influenced by
other powerful forces — some of them new. I have in mind,
for example, the consumer movement, the environmen-
talists, the other members of the EEC, as well as, of course,
the press, the trade unions, the CBI and academics and so
on. These organisations have a separate existence from the
three original members of our trinity and they can often
impose constraints on the activities of individuals,
enterprises, and the state; they also influence our
expectations and the way we think.

DOE: the microcosm

So far I have suggested three potent influences: the force of
ideas, the tide of expectation and the influence of other
dimensions including the international lobbies, interest
groups and the media. How do these forces interact? What
is the relationship between the state, the individual and the
enterprise? Is the relationship changing and can we foresee
what changes the future will bring? I would like to suggest
some answers — or at least some clues — to these questions
by relating them for a short period to the work of the
Department of the Environment.

What, you may ask, is the DOE? When the Department
was first formed in 1970, that very question was being
debated by two clergymen. 'Easy', said one of them, 'the
Department of the Environment must deal with everything
which is not the result of heredity'.

In fact DOE is responsible, under its Ministers, for the formation and supervision of national policies on housing, land use, the structure and finance of local government, water and the environment generally. Until a month ago, the Secretary of State for the Environment was also responsible for transport policy but this is now the concern of the Secretary of State for Transport, with whose Department the new slimmer line DOE shares offices, common citizenship and common services — such as organisation, planning, economics, statistics, research etc. The two Departments will continue to work very closely together so as to ensure that the links between planning, transport and housing are taken into account in formulating policy. The distinctive feature of the policy forming responsibilities of the DOE is that implementation lies mainly with outside bodies, notably local government. We are, in this respect, a series of conduits through which money and advice flow to the bodies with executive responsibilities.

DOE is also a regulatory body; for example the Secretary of State makes the building regulations.

We are also an appellate body. For example, our Ministers decide planning appeals.

Moreover, DOE provides services — for example, the Property Services Agency designs and provides office and other accommodation for all government departments and the armed forces. Then, too, we are in the tourist business, through our responsibilities for ancient monuments and historic buildings, such as Stonehenge and the Tower of London. You will sleep safer in your beds for the knowledge that the care of the Crown Jewels rests in our hands.

DOE is a social Department, like the Department of Health and Social Security; but we are also an economic Department because so much of our work — directly or indirectly — affects industry and the way the nation's resources are used. For example, in 1975/76 public expenditure on the services for which DOE is responsible amounted to over £8,000 million. And our Ministers' decisions have a major impact on the use of national resources. It is interesting to look at public expenditure for housing and transport in 1971 and to look at the projections for those two services in 1981: the immense swing, rightly or wrongly, from transport to housing. On top of its social and economic functions, DOE is the sponsoring Department for local Government. If my Department does not look after local democracy, I can assure you no other Department of central Government will. And we are too, I suppose in a sense, the Department for the Quality of Life — again I repeat if we do not try and look after the environment, who else will? DOE illustrates the pervasiveness of the state in contemporary British life.

I have not talked about DOE at such length in order to get the Department a commercial in peak time, but because I believe DOE illustrates in microcosm most of the contemporary features of the relationship between the State, the enterprise and the individual.

Clean air

Take, for example, clean air. Pollution of the atmosphere is not, of course, a new preoccupation. Our old friend John Evelyn wrote in 1661 that:

> 'It is this horrid smoke which obscures our Churches, and makes our Palaces look old, which fouls our clothes and corrupts the Waters, so as the very Rain and refreshing Dews which fall in the several seasons precipitate this impure vapour, which, in its black and tenacious quality, spoils and contaminates whatever is exposed to it'.

During the last century and the first half of this one there was increasing interest by Parliament in cleaning up the atmosphere. The objective of this was to protect public health and property from the worst excesses of air pollution.

1952 marks a watershed in our thinking. You will remember that in December of that year we had a fearful smog which covered London for five days. There was an immediate increase in both illness and death. Indeed, it has been suggested that 4000 people died because of the smog. Result: the Beaver Committee was set up and their work led to the passage of the Clean Air Act 1956.

Notice the title: *not* Abatement of Pollution or Public Health or Smoke Control. No. *Clear Air* was the title and the intention. The sort of fires in our homes, the fuel we use on them, the height of furnace chimneys, all these were and are now regulated. Why did this come about? Because of the force of an idea — that clean air is a right — and because of higher expectations about what individuals, enterprises and the state can legitimately be required to do in the public interest.

There is no doubt that the clean air requirements add to the costs of manufacturers and perhaps of households too. They also curtail individual freedom of action. But the alternative is smog, more illness, higher death rates and a general reduction in the quality of life. There was and remains a consensus that the state should step in to regulate the activities of individuals and enterprises so as to ensure clean air in the public interest. Regulation of this sort is one of the classic roles of ministeries such as DOE and is a characteristic of the modern state. The knack, of course, is to strike the right balance between control and higher costs, on the one hand, and pollution and anarchy, on the other.

And it is here that the state seems likely to come into conflict with the enterprise and the individual (or associations claiming to speak for him). Cut down one problem and a hundred spring up in its place. To anyone who can remember what the old 'pea-soupers' were like, it seems that we have overcome the worst of our air pollution problems. 'Not enough' cry many individuals. 'What about aerosols, lead in petrol and asbestos particles?' And it is the case, for example, aerosols and lead in petrol do undoubtedly cause pollution.

But do these and other such features of life today present sufficient of a threat to warrant state intervention, which would be bound to put up manufacturing costs, send some firms broke, and interfere with private enterprise? Alas for the state, most of the easy black or white decisions have been taken. We are now well into the grey areas, pushed there by higher expectations and an increasingly voluble and well-educated — though sometimes only partially informed — general public. On the one hand stand those whose lives are made unpleasant by the muck of some industry, supported by the growing number of people concerned with the standards of the environment; on the other hand, there are the considerations of national economic growth, industrial costs and entrepreneurial freedom.

Development control

Certainly, there are many businessmen who believe that we have not struck a satsifactory balance between these two sets of considerations so far as the control of the development of land is concerned. Some critics say that the way the planning system currently works is harmful not only to private enterprise but also to the regeneration of British industry.

Yet the development control system is based on impeccable foundations. An individual's or an enterprise's wish to develop land in a particular way could have intolerable effects on other individuals, business or the community at large. The purpose of planning is to regulate the development and use of land in the public interest; it is not actually concerned to protect the private interests of one person against the activities of another. But the material question is not whether owners of neighbouring properties would suffer financial loss, but whether the proposal would affect the locality generally and lead to a change in its character which would be contrary to the public interest.

Anyone who has visited the older towns in parts of the United States can see for himself the mess and unsightly squalor which can result where there is no effective control over development. But even twenty years ago many people in this country — not just in commerce and industry but individuals too — regarded planners and planning as a gross intrusion in their personal freedom.

It seems to me that the situation has changed radically so that now there is a real division between the way development control is regarded by enterprises and the way private individuals — or at least an important group of them — see it. What has happened, I think, is that some of the most able and articulate members of the community have come to the conclusion that by skilful manipulation of the development control machine, they can be pretty effective in preventing — or at least delaying — any planning proposals which they think would make any change at all in the appearance or life of the area they live in.

It is, of course, welcome and important that people should care enough about their communities to want to influence the development of their areas. But there are also some worrying features. For example, some people already believe that the development control system puts too many obstacles in the way of any change, no matter what the cost to the economy or enterprise. Moreover, the delay, expense and frustration which both enterprise and individuals perceive to be among the features of the development control system can bring them into conflict with the state.

On matters such as pollution and development control, the role of the state is, of course, to try to relate social and environmental considerations to those of an industrial and economic nature, so as to discern where the public interest — the balance between these two sets of considerations — really lies. Often the state seems unable to satisfy either camp and is highly successful in disappointing both of them. The danger of this is that both sides may increasingly come to regard the state as either their enemy or as an impotent and expensive muddler. How can we avoid this?

Public participation

In fact, we cannot and indeed it might be dangerous if people in this country were to learn to 'kiss the rod'. A dislike for government is probably a very healthy thing and I believe most people would still agree with Tom Paine that: 'Government, even in its best state, is but a necessary evil: in its worst, an intolerable one'.

I think one should accept, therefore, that any government in this country is not going to be popular if it is worth its salt. Perhaps the Civil Service Commissioners should publicise the fact that only masochists should apply for entry to the government service. As Thomas Hooker said: 'He that goeth about to persuade a multitude that they are not so well governed as they ought to be, shall never want attentive and favourable hearers'.

But while we can afford the maturity which accepts that no-one who wants to win a beauty contest goes into government, we cannot afford to sit back and accept the alienation of the electorate from the democratic process.

I think it is partly this anxiety — the feeling that we must ensure that the gap between those in authority both centrally and locally and those under it is not allowed to widen — that lies behind the trend we have seen over the last decade towards public participation. Through the participation procedures, the state tries to give people information about the problem to be tackled, the resources available and the comparative merits of the options. In return, the state seeks the views and wishes of those affected by the problems, be they individuals or enterprises. But information is not the end of the story. People are also interested in *how* decisions are taken and in the *attitudes* of those who take the decisions. For example, some people are questioning the impartiality and objectivity of government departments in the exercise of appellate functions (over, say, planning decisions) in quite a new way. Public participation may be one way of recognising this interest in the 'how' and the 'who' of making decisions.

Another reason for the trend towards participation is, I suspect, the raising of the general level of education, the demise of the deference and fear people used to have for their 'betters', the force of ideas, and higher expectations. All of these seem to me to have brewed up to produce an increasingly pervasive belief that people have more *right* to be involved in government than they used to have. I wonder if you would agree that people are nowhere near so content to leave matters entirely to their elected leaders — be they MPs, councillors, trades union officials or the CBI — as they were during, say, the '50s.

Participation is heady stuff and is still in its infancy. I believe it can be a very effective force for better government and greater justice in this country. But there does seem to be a risk that it could lead to waste and frustration in some cases unless individuals, firms and government departments learn to adapt to it. Indeed I think we also need to clarify what we mean by 'participation'. There influence decisions and that, I think, is likely to remain a minority interest, pursued mainly by the more articulate members of the community. The second element concerns the wish, which I believe all of us share, for better access to those in central and local government who have authority over, say, our assessment for tax, or how much sickness benefit we get when we are ill, or why the road outside our houses is being dug up and so on. Finding one's way through the official labyrinth seems to many to be a trial fit for Hercules. I am sure that firms, as well as individuals, would regard it as a great step forward if they could find out quickly and simply who in government to get in touch with when they have a question or a problem. In other words ought we to be providing some better maps to the labyrinth?

What seems reasonably clear is that participation, whether broadly or narrowly defined, is here to stay. In the process, I suggest we shall have to answer some hard questions about the process and accessibility of government as well as about the distribution of power and responsibility within the community.

Industrial democracy

Just as some people are demanding a more direct say about the way in which they are governed, they are also asserting a right to a say in the control of employment and production. This is part of the reason for the pressure for industrial democracy and the calls for consumers to have a voice in the management of public and private industries.

Just as the participation movement requires us to take a hard look at the way we traditionally regard our institutions of government so the industrial democracy and consumer movements pose questions about the relationships between the managements of business enterprises and their employees and customers.

Of course, some managements have already established new relationships with their workers and consumers. But others either reject the notion of industrial democracy or believe it to be unworkable on the terms advocated by many trades unions. The state has an interest in this for two main reasons: first, because of its general responsibilities for the economy and industrial relations; and, second, because there are demands for the government to force firms to bring workers into the management and control of the business.

Private enterprise is not, of course, alone in having to grapple with the complex question posed by industrial democracy. In part, this is because one cannot build a corral round and say that everything in that corral is private enterprise and is different from all the activities outside it. For example, where does one draw the line between a private firm and, say, British Leyland? It is only a step from British Leyland to Cable and Wireless; and from there to the nationalised industries. Once into the public sector, local authorities and central government itself must be involved. As Ministers told Parliament last February 1976: 'Industrial democracy in the public sector presents special problems because of the role of Parliament and local authorities as representatives of the electorate. It is fundamental to the working of democracy as we know it that elected representatives take decisions and act in the interests of the community as a whole; that principle cannot be breached. But, within the need to preserve the accountability of elected representatives and the requirements of the public interest, employees and their representatives in the public services should be given the maximum opportunity to contribute their views on matters of legitimate staff interest'. Accordingly, in parallel with the work of the Bullock Committee which is considering industrial democracy in the private sector, studies are going on, in consultation with unions and managements. into the scope for the extension of industrial democracy throughout the public services, including central and local government. The intention is that these studies should be completed in time for the Government to be able to take an overall view of the private and public sectors after the Bullock Committee has reported.

I am not, of course, going to make any predictions about what the outcome of all these studies is likely to be. The reason I have spoken about industrial democracy is that it seems to me to be a particularly good illustration of the dynamic nature of that relationship between the state, the enterprise and the individual and the impact of the force of an idea on that relationship.

Prosperity industrial strategy

What I am confident is beyond dispute is that prosperity is an aim shared by all three members of our trinity. Upon the regeneration of British industry depend the maintenance and improvement of individuals' standards of living, the success and fulfilment of firms and their managers and the creation of the wealth necessary to finance social programmes for the community's benefit.

Such has been the speed of change in our thinking since the war that there is now virtual unanimity that we can achieve prosperity only through co-operation between the government, the private sector, the trade unions and individual workers. Through the Industrial Strategy and the National Enterprise Board, the state is now involved in — indeed, many firms have invited the government into — areas formerly thought to be none of its business.

DOE has an important contribution to make to the success of the Industrial Strategy and so has local government. Our activities in relation to land-use, building standards, pollution and so on have a direct effect on manufacturing costs and industrial development. Our aim is to do our work in such a way that we encourage and support industry rather than hinder it with a thousand bureaucratic pin-pricks.

But — and it is a vital but — we must guard against letting out the baby with the bath water. Buildings last for a long time. It might well be very wasteful to permit construction which would be outmoded within ten to fifteen years. Moreover, it is easier to destroy our countryside that to recreate it. Indeed, very often the change is irreversible.

We must operate, therefore, on the margin, on the balance between industrial and other considerations. I would not claim that the balance is perfect at the moment. For example, I should like to see the system for giving decisions on planning applications speeded up and simplified and, with the help of local government, I believe this should be possible. But we shall not improve the balance unless developers — enterprise — accept that the state is not just bloody-minded — or not invariably — and give local authorities and government departments clear and early warning of their intentions and needs.

The diffusion of power

Leaping swiftly from that possibly provocative remark, perhaps I could say a little about the way in which the British Constitution seems to have been changing so that the exercise of power has become more diffuse and complex. The conventional picture is, of course, that Britain has two great organs of power — Parliament and the Government. But bodies such as the TUC, the CBI and the National Economic Development Council now have an

important voice in the way the country is governed.
Parliament is generally thought to have become less
important than it used to be. One has got to be aware of the
possible dangers of milking away power and authority from
the Parliamentary process into appointed agencies, into
hived-off bodies. It will be interesting, too, how the EEC
develops over the next decade — it cannot remain static and
all of us will be affected by these developments.

On top of that, it is proposed that there should be elected
Assemblies for Scotland and Wales and there are demands
for devolution to strong elected regional bodies in England.
While I am reeling off this list of the bodies which already
are or may become parts of the state, we should not, of
course, forget our county councils, district councils, parish
councils, water authorities, the National Health Authorities
and so on. Some may believe we are a touch overgoverned.

The all-pervasive state

In many way, we have already reached the point where the
state is regarded as having, if not a responsibility for, at least
an interest in all aspects of British economic and social life.
Employers often protest at the extent of government
intervention but, when problems arise, often regard the
state as having a duty to solve them. For example, some
firms insisted that it was the government's responsibility
not only to ensure they got sufficient water to continue
production but also that the additional cost of providing it
during the drought should be met by the tax payer.

Individuals are no less ambivalent in their attitude to the
state. On the one hand, many resent the chore of
completing census forms. But they expect new schools,
hospitals and houses to be built at the right time and in the
right place and criticise ministers if, through lack of
information, they make mistakes. Moreover, there are some

who say the government should provide free sites — even subsidies — for pop concerts, should legislate to require the provision of lavatories for dogs or bring in a bill to make people walk on the left hand side of the pavement.

Is there, then, nothing which the government should not regulate or control?

Conclusion

Earlier, I said that although political philosophers were unable to agree about the nature of the relationship between the state, the enterprise and the individual, there is general agreement that there are certain human rights — freedom of association, freedom of movement and so on.

This poses a number of interesting questions. Should there be a clear limitation on the activities of the state? Should it be precluded from taking action — except in times of national emergency — which could infringe human rights? Should the state's job be to ensure that these rights are upheld and to act against individuals, enterprises or any organisation which seeks to curtail those rights?

One possibility, as Sir Leslie Scarman and Lord Hailsham have suggested, might be to enact some sort of Bill of Rights and to create, in effect, a Constitutional Court, which could challenge not only the activities of the government but the legislation approved by Parliament. But perhaps a Bill of Rights would be just one more complication — more law, more litigation, more frustration and further complication.

If a Bill of Rights is one possibility, perhaps a greater emphasis on efficiency might be another. One of the great strengths of this country is that people are not frightened of the government and have no hesitation about expressing their views and criticisms. Indeed, the British have a genius for organising themselves into voluntary associations in order to press their particular sectional interests — be they anti-vivisection, abortion law reform, industrial democracy or whatever. The freedom and — despite what one sometimes hears — the great tolerance in this country makes it a good place to live in and this is often forgotten when we are bemoaning our economic performance.

I believe we should accept and, indeed, welcome people's willingness to voice their wishes and to organise themselves to try to get the state to act as the sectional interests want. But perhaps the state needs to be more effective in identifying and stating in public how the measures proposed by one sectional interest would affect the rest of the community and what would have to be foregone, and by whom, if any particular new benefit were introduced. Perhaps we — all of us — need to become a bit more realistic about how much difference we really make when we tinker with the machinery of government. Perhaps we are too prone to set up yet another *ad hoc* body — to advise or co-ordinate or regulate — without being sufficiently clear about how effective the new machinery will be and in what way it will be accountable to the community at large. Sometimes it seems, to me, we duck the deep-seated difficult policy decisions and alter the structure instead.

My point is simply this. The relationship between the state, the enterprise and the individual is a dynamic one. The period since 1945 has been one in which expectations have risen faster than ever before and many new and potent ideas have come into circulation. These expectations and ideas have affected the relationship between the government, private enterprise and the citizen. Our critical economic situation is forcing us to take stock of the way in which the relationship has developed over the last thirty years. And I think that this is hopeful because, in the process of overcoming our economic difficulties, we may see both a resolution of some of the conflicts to be found within the current relationship between the state, the enterprise and the individuals, and also some simplification of the machinery which has grown up around it.

10 Is Britain becoming a corporate state?

W.L. Weinstein

Fellow and Tutor in Politics, Balliol College since 1962 Bill Weinstein was previously Research Fellow of the Social Science Research Council in New York and Nuffield College, Oxford. He has also been a Visiting Fellow in the Institute of Advanced Studies in the Australian National University and Visiting Lecturer at the Makerere University, Uganda. He has written widely on Liberty and his current interests include the political aspects of management authority and conflict, the social responsibility of business, and communication between business and education. He is a Visiting Fellow of the Oxford Management Centre.

This essay springs directly from the British context. Its argumentative contours, empirical material, historical references, implicit assumptions and style of discourse all testify to this fact. I should therefore begin with an apology for the relative parochialism of my remarks. To those who are not from the UK, and to both those who are and are not but nevertheless find tiresome the current obsessions of a country descending noisily down the back and dimly-lit staircase towards historical obscurity, I can only plead for your forebearance.

Although I could argue that what is important in the analysis of UK problems is genuinely relevant to other countries, at any rate to those that are also advanced industrial, it would be absurd to insist that the UK describes or prefigures the economic and political patterns of other countries. Too many of her infirmities as well as remaining points of strength derive from a specific, perhaps unique, economic, cultural and political history. The representation of the present structure of the UK, which is much of my task on this occasion, is perhaps nothing more than the model of the UK alone, rather than the model of post-industrial society as such. Nevertheless the struggle to comprehend her present and future may be more widely relevant, especially as it involves the use of political and social concepts and hypotheses that could be applied with modification outside the UK. Indeed I shall examine one kind of general concept — 'corporatism', together with its associated ideas of corporate society and corporate state. These ideas, with some risks, can be applied to more than one society.

I am a political philosopher. This ivory-towerish title usually carries portentous implications: a tendency towards the clouds and misty realms of reflection on human ideals and principles, and contemplation of a perfect and static world of refined conceptualisations and utopian aspirations which are removed from the rough, real world.

On this occasion, however, I am attempting a partial role-reversal by addressing myself fully, not to the world as it ought to be, but as it is. The reversal is only partial after all, for not only personally have I long tried to study contemporary societies, it is a well-established and continuing practice among political philosophers to depict the world as it is. Moreover, they may have a special role in this observational enterprise directed at the real world; for that task is more difficult that it seems at first. The social world does not present itself ready-made, like the objects of physical perception. And even those objects, like chairs or the sun's rays, require a language, discursive and mathematical, if they are to be understood and interrelated. More troublesome is the fact that the social world, unlike the physical, is even partly constituted by people's concepts and their beliefs about it. What they understand of it, however, imperfectly makes much of the real social world what it is, and provides the analyst with a starting point. Furthermore, understanding of the social world through observation is mediated by our concepts. The description, explanation and interpretation of things as they are is therefore governed by conceptual and methodological issues which it is appropriate for the political philosopher to contend with. And this is as true as when he stands at the elbow of men of action as when he retreats to his own ivory tower.

This preliminary point is reinforced by a contemporary consideration. It is virtually a truism that, when social reality is stable and secure, the political philosopher has little to say of direct practical relevance. Without his help ordinary people find their own pragmatically adequate ways of understanding and coping. But when times are swiftly changing and unsteady, indeed vertiginous, as they are now, people's struggle — especially in groups whose positions and assumptions are threatened by change — to find an orientation to their world clamours for the attention of the political philosopher. And so far as all of us are concerned, there is at such times an urgent need to develop and deploy concepts that help to bridge the gap between a disintegrating present and an uncertain future. He naturally gravitates towards the realities, believing that, unless he can interpret the actual world, possibly the cultivation of his analytical skills is of little practical worth to anyone — worth no more perhaps than the kind of private indulgence that may come of pursuing a hobby. I need therefore hardly explain further the import of my own involvement in the Oxford Centre for Management Studies. However, having said this I quickly and insistently disclaim pretensions to superior comprehension. In fact at several points it will emerge how blunt and cumbersome are the intellectual instruments of political analysis when used to confront the world as it is.

I shall outline the concepts of corporatism and their relevance to the present UK situation, and at various points try to mould them to the complex reality which they can barely capture. Indeed the descriptive adequacy of concepts of corporatism, each of uncertain content and variable application, is rightly to be questioned. More generally, our political language is so inadequate in depicting realistically *types* of political society — e.g. democracy, socialism, liberalism (and various hybrids of these three), representative government, autocracy, authoritarianism, totalitarianism, dictatorship, tyranny, fascism, and so on — that it is almost a mistake to embark on an inquiry into present realities with any expectation that corporatism could be a more helpful concept than any other.

Let me nevertheless proceed in the spirit of the chef who, with the various ingredients of a potentially wholesome meal laid out, suppresses his nervousness over the outcome. The concept of corporatism cannot be ignored; it is now widely in use in politics, and has received academic support (J.T. Winkler, 'Law, State and Economy: The Industry Act

1975 in Context', *British Journal of Law and Society*, volume 12, number 2, 1975; and R.E. Pahl & J.T. Winkler, 'Corporatism in Britain', *The Times*, 26 March 1976). Indeed there seems to be an irreducible place for master-concepts, themselves highly complex and synthetic, such as liberal, or by complete or partial contrast, corporate, political society. For all their difficulty, they may help to illuminate in outline the changing relations between the individual, the enterprise and the state — and to call attention to the changing meanings of these three categories. In the last resort, however, one ought not to worry about how I shall use the labels but instead one might focus on what is being put underneath them.

I

The very concept 'corporate' or 'corporation' implies types of social organisation which unite or bind people together in some continuing way, voluntarily or coercively. It suggests collective action and purpose, at least in theory if not in practice. It has therefore operated as a term in contrast with two other phenomena: a market society in which independent individuals interact through contracts as decision-making units, or a non-market society under the sway of an oligarchy or monarchy whose power does not rest on or could not be checked by intermediate social groups designated as corporations. It is easy to see that in present contexts to speak of a corporate *society* is to refer to the specific economic entity, a type of business organisation, which has reduced the scope for perfect competition among individual or small-group producers. This use of the term is quite unproblematic, though it has now been extended to other economic organisations such as trade-unions and employers' associations. In fact 'corporate society' now can imply that in all major fields of human activity, in education, politics, the arts, religion and production, the capacity of individuals to interact as relatively independent and unattached social atoms has been diminished, and in their place are large-scale organisations controlling the bulk of resources, communications and options that are available to particular individuals.

There is no doubt that the UK and industrial societies generally, though still harbouring a plurality of corporate bodies, are dominated more than ever by the idea and the reality of corporatism, by the integration of multitudes within large-scale organisations. The concept of corporatism *in society* therefore depicts the changed position of the individual, and focusses on the distribution of power and resources within society, and in the case of multinational corporations, across national boundaries. But on its face 'corporate society' says nothing about the powers and functions of the state. There might be a powerful array of corporate bodies in society, economic, religious and educational, and a relatively weak or limited state; or a state whose powers permeate and even subjugate the various corporate bodies in society. So whether or not one sees, for example, the modern manager-run, rather than owner-run, business corporation as maximising profits or *satisficing*, its existence for more than a century has raised controversial issues over the individual's relation to it, as both employee and consumer, and its relation to other corporate entitites as well as the 'total corporation' of the body politic.

By contrast, ideas about the corporate *state* have an older lineage, though some of them parallel the development of the business corporation. Almost all ideas about state corporatism have roots in one kind of political ideology or another. For example, one important kind of corporate-state thinking was inspired by hostility towards late eighteenth and early nineteenth century liberal ideas of free contract, the free market in property, the dependence of wealth production upon a multiplicity of individual and small units, as well as political claims to free thought and association, and limited, responsible and representative government. This kind of corporatism dramatised the disunity, fragmentation, selfishness and overt conflict that mark a liberal order. In contrast with liberalism, which sharply distinguished between state and society, and conceived the state merely as an umpire or 'night-watchman', imposing minimum rules over social activities while within that loose framework individuals and groups could freely pursue their own good in their own way, corporate-state theories often called for an organic unity of society and for consensus expressed in the state's development of a centralised strategy for the whole society. These theories harked back to pre-market, hierarchically-ordered societies or looked forward to a policy which developed positive goals untainted by liberalism's scepticism about the validity of any collective goals, especially those which left opaque what kind of good the individual was supposed to derive from them. The state, in alliance with either religion or some new social science, was to bring about the organic unity of society — by contrast with the second-rate, mechanical and precarious unity of a free market which left too much to an ill-founded faith in the rationality and goodness of free-wheeling individuals.

Not suprisingly such state corporatism had adherents at very diverse points of the ideological spectrum. There were left-wing critics of a class-divided, no-longer Christian society; in the name of social science Comte looked forward to a harmonious society governed by planners and technocrats; and later in France from the liberal camp itself there evolved a loosely allied group known as 'solidaristes' who emphasised, not individual competition but curbs on it, not individual rights but individual debts and duties to society. In British experience the preference for state technocracy and management over the free play of market forces was expressed by the Fabians.

On the right, the Catholic Church in the nineteenth

century, for example, in its invectives against Godless materialism and the individualism of the market on the one hand, and socialism's conception of class war springing from and destroying a market society together with religion itself, developed a doctrine of corporatism which espoused unifying and shared goals for all, especially employers and employees. Nearer to our own day, Italian fascism was a self-styled corporate state, as was Salazar's Portugal, which sought to integrate coercively many social organisations under party and state. Nazism suppressed the independence of the working-class organisations, religious and other groups in the name of racial unity; one of its professed goals was to gear all activity to higher purposes, to infuse unity into a divided people through a doctrine of racial-cum-national strength. All this goes to show that the ideological roots of modern state corporatism are diverse, though there may be a common theme, sometimes starkly visible as a hostility towards the alleged disunity and futile conflict of liberal society.

In recent decades, however, corporate-state thinking has been distinguished in other ways. On the other hand, as a crude generalisation, there is a French style of state corporatism denoted, not accidentally, by French terms in our language: *étatiste* and *dirigiste*. Possibly its source of inspiration comes from the policies of two directors of French state finance in the seventeenth century, Mazarin and Colbert. In pursuit of domestic objectives such as breaking the power of regional noblemen and conducting a royal tax-grab, and international objectives such as France's economic autarchy, government would protect French industries and stimulate investment. However this is still a long way from ideas about state-determined priorities in terms of which society would be re-fashioned and forced or encouraged to develop economically. In fact we would have to look to seventeenth and eighteenth century examples of Russian and Prussian monarchical modernisation policies to find more full-blooded cases of state corporatism, involving economic goal-setting, state control of resources, and suppression of internal conflict for the sake of high-level power strategies.

On the other hand, state corporatism might involve a very diluted form of state control combined with pluralism. The eighteenth and nineteenth centuries provide numerous examples, in France or Prussia or Britain, of governments stimulating growth through favourable charters and licenses granted to private investors. In our own time pluralistic corporation seeks to involve business and other groups through negotiation and consent; mechanisms of conflict-resolution are created, but co-operation is voluntary and not geared to a great national plan. Corporatism of this type still limits freedom of individuals and institutions; it is not *laissez-faire,* but its easy rein implies that the depth and scope of state direction of the economy are decidedly checked by the counter-powers of economic blocs, and that parliamentary government gives significant expression to the diffusion of power.

We have therefore, as a broad contrast, a corporate state which is highly activist, extensive in its controls and tending towards a monopoly of power and one which is held in check by an array of independent economic associations. In either case there might be present or absent another feature frequently associated with the corporate state: the official representation through national syndicates of various industrial or occupational groups, such 'functional' representation superceding the system based on geographical constituencies. Whether any such corporate representation does provide a sufficient index of the distribution of power is an open question, for it could be a mere facade.

II

With these remarks as background we can quickly grasp the content and politically emotive overtones of recent attempts to bring 'corporate state' into the common currency of British politics. No doubt we could start to detect signs of a trend towards state corporatism, but the important question is, which kind? One obvious sign is the blurring of distinctions, once thought to be clearer, between public and private enterprises because of their close interdependence and interpenetration. Indeed it is no longer so self-evident that modern liberal democracies respect a boundary between the public and the private in practice; they may therefore slide unwittingly towards a situation which totalitarian regimes try to bring about.

One appeal of the idea of state corporatism therefore seems to be its explanatory use; instead of using the worn-out, cast-iron distinctions of liberalism, it supercedes them by ceasing to classify enterprises as either essentially public or private. That distinction remains more notional than real. Instead, then, the state emerges as the Great Entrepreneur, competing for resources against other enterprises, while legally embracing many of these enterprises itself. The state is seen as a Janus-faced Friend/ Foe, alternatively Facilitator and Frustrator. The level of taxation on company profits and unearned incomes, not to mention other revenues, makes the state itself the Great Rentier in society, a concept hitherto reserved for a type of capitalist in the 'private' sector.

The appeal of the concept is enhanced when one notes the way the British state had perforce to shift from a supportive role in the economy, marked by sporadic interventions and withdrawals, to a more sustained and directive role. Much of this has occured as a response to momentous historical trends or events — the struggle of the economy to succeed or survive against the rise of America,

Germany and Japan, the historic run-down in the investment base and decades of low productivity, the costs and strains of two total wars and the inter-war slump, the collapse and disappearance of the world's largest empire, and the growth of the welfare state.

All these have been general factors lying behind what some commentators regard as a trend towards a strong corporate state. Many of them see this as produced neither by design (e.g. the fulfilment of a socialist strategy) nor by mere accident — but by largely uncontrolled and perhaps still uncontrollable forces, such as the changing balance of international economic power. Some commentators see the trend as a mutation arising from the business society itself; out of opportunism or a justifiable sense of precariousness, businesses have sought government aid such as cheap credit. They have played a risky game with government, treating it as a market resource or milch-cow while being scathing about its tax demands or the stupidity of politicians and civil servants.

Behind this lies, of course, perception of the role of the big battalions, the Trades Union Congress, the Confederation of British Industry, employers' federations and trade associations, and the development of intimate, if tense, relationships between government, TUC and CBI, through which economic policies are nationalised and all negotiating parties are in effect the co-authors of what is still officially termed 'Government' policy. Behind this appreciation of the situation lies another: the historical trend towards concentration of capital assets and market shares in fewer and larger enterprises. It is sometimes pointed out that the typical response of British companies since at least 1900, when faced with adversity, has been to opt for mergers and take-overs — not as aggressive, expansive tactics but as self-protective, conserving ones. Whatever the diagnoses, there are large concentrations of power in many markets. It is therefore argued that the realities of free competition have disappeared in the domestic economy, and with them the very basis on which profitability provides a test of the efficient use of resources — thereby undermining the legitimacy of the private sector. The reality of the state/economy division has also largely disappeared, and the state, in the strong version of corporatism, emerges as a kind of central directorate of a national conglomerate, starkly evident in the area of defence expenditure and with growing evidence in the energy and high-technology industries. Such trends, it may be argued, are even reflected in the fact that the traditional division in trade-union circles between 'industrial' and 'political' issues has been breaking down.

State corporatism as an explanatory and predictive tool has today in Britain a striking appeal. It signifies at least a proper scepticism over the utility of master-concepts inherited from an earlier epoch. To simplify matters, I shall spell out what may crudely be called a 'strong' thesis about the corporate state which has been advanced in recent years. According to this strong thesis the state aims for an organic unity of individuals and associations, and their submission or subordination to its overriding goals. The individual's role is to conform, and to acquire his personal indentity through his corporate affiliations in the work-place and his acceptance of the nation's economic goals. Common goals and shared interests are to override sectional and selfish ones. If this does not involve the Nazi idea of *Gleichschaltung*, the transformation through subversion and suppression of independent organisations into a unified transmission-belt for the implementation of grand strategies, it is a close-knit partnership of elites under the overall direction of the state for the sake of national economic success. The goals appear to emerge from consent and voluntary agreement, but are often coercively imposed or areas of negotiation are severely constrained. The state is thus the supreme wielder of commands and incentives, changing their mix in response to changes in the situation.

There is much in this picture that managers and directors of enterprises could start to accept as realistic. For having been at the receiving end of major changes in the balance of power and objectives in society, they can readily identify through daily experience the ways in which their prerogatives have been diminished. In the spheres of industrial relations — pay, de-manning, hiring, working conditions, union recognition — of disclosure of information, of dividends, taxation, investment, reorganisation and acquisition, the restriction and devolution of managerial powers have become one way of defining the trend towards a corporate state. Going further, there is perceived an unholy alliance between government and unions, and a radical undermining of incentives through recent land and tax legislation. Managerial rewards themselves have been squeezed; questions about government direction of more investment are being taken seriously; national threshold agreements on pay are bargained against food price supports and dividend controls; the pursuit of private goods in a free market is increasingly replaced by the pursuit of collective goods through planning and controls; each attempt to co-ordinate economic policy leads to fresh demands to co-ordinate a wider field of variables because one thing depends on another and can upset the best of plans; and among the responsibilities loaded upon government is the duty to protect or compensate the cost-bearers of economic change. For the mechanisms of the economic market, whether or not workable, there are increasingly substituted public mechanisms, political and bureaucratic, for resource allocation. Political power, which few managers see themselves possessing, has become a critical variable in economic decision-making.

To the historical realist another appeal of the corporate

state concept is that it is not uniquely or even strongly associated with a movement to socialism. Socialist ideas and movements are one kind of ingredient in the multi-sided trend towards corporatism. In reality the alleged movement to socialism may reflect rather than cause more basic historical pressures towards state (or state-plus-big battalions) control over the economy, and these pressures are as strongly manifested when Conservatives are in office as when they are not. Socialist ideology, in other words, contributes to a trend which will not result in socialism but something else: a corporate state which is neither liberal nor socialist, neither recognisably capitalist nor anything else. The objective significance of leftism in Britain is not achievement of its goals — except perhaps one goal which many on the left have not disavowed consistently, namely, the abolition of a liberal society. If this analysis is correct, the depth of the tragedy which it depicts restrains the temptation to engage in light-hearted remarks about the ironical twists of history.

A further feature of the strong version of state corporatism is that it deliberately de-emphasizes the post-war notion of a 'mixed economy' with its implication that the most informative distinction is that between a nationalised sector and a privately-owned sector which co-exist under the umbrella of government monetary and fiscal policies. Whilst conceding the residual elements of reality in this picture, the strong version of corporate state sees no significant increase in official public ownership, but a significant increase in the depth, range and type of government control over privately-owned business and a significant change in the philosophy behind government involvement in the economy. The private sector in this scenario comes under increasingly detailed surveillance and control. The provision of collective goods through market forces is rejected in favour of government directives, decrees and initiatives; goal-setting comes from the top, through direct collaboration of the leaderships of union, private and public capital, and the government. The circles of control widen to relate resource allocation to the distribution of rewards, and this happens both before and after government-sponsored inquiries into the reward system (e.g. *Reports of the Royal Commission on the Distribution of Income and Wealth*, 1975, 1976). Increasingly the state goes in for control over sectors of industry, not merely over industry in general. As what once seemed like temporary, short-run expedients for coping with specific problems harden into durable policies and institutionalised relations and controls, it would seem that the idea of a corporate state cuts across and supercedes the idea of a mixed economy as an explanatory and predicitve device.

This conviction is reinforced as the state attempts further to control basic industries, to co-ordinate supplies and services, such as machine-tools, energy and land; or as it injects capital in high-priority manufacturing industries and adopts serious controls over the movement of capital. Another projected move, planning agreements, gives both government and unions a more detailed voice in business policy. All this, though covered by legislation, may erode the legal system: binding decisions and social order derive not from the law but from a corporatist ethos of common interests and co-operation; legal codification is superceded by direct administrative and political interventions which are basically discretionary.

The overall philosophy, as Winkler describes it, is to impose unity, to achieve national economic success and internal order by undermining the competitive scramble for scarce resources. Perhaps the gist of the idea is that a strong corporate state sets macro-objectives, develops much consequential intervention through commands and controlled incentives, and determines through an integrated political-administrative process the difficult trade-offs between productive efficiency, equality and liberty.

However as my next set of remarks will make clear, what

is crucial is not what the state intends to do, but by what process and in what context economic objectives will be set and implemented. How closed or open the process will or could be is a critical issue. This is what I shall now focus upon. But broad as that issue may be, behind it lurks another, even larger in scale, which I can only mention, not go into: *if* we are moving towards a strong corporate state is that merely a symptom of profound instability in the present system, in which case such a state is doomed to break down itself — or is such a state necessary for the stability of a system which can be stabilised after all?

III

Appealing as the strong thesis about the corporate state may be, there are several good reasons for holding that Britain is not such a state. It so far manifests a highly imperfect, ill-coordinated and incomplete kind of political corporatism which is nearer to the pluralist than the monolithic and unified pole of corporatism. We are still a highly pluralistic society and state; unified is what we are not.

But as we are a corporate society, and the state as well as corporate bodies wield power over the individual, the fears of liberals are not unjustified. If I deny that we are clearly on-course towards a strong corporate state, then it does not follow that we have splendid opportunities to sustain or become a more liberal society. There is a middle which should not be excluded. There is a messier and more moderate characterisation available: neither the liberalism of the free economics and politics, nor strong state corporatism. My historical snap-shot of Britian is more problematic, suggesting a moderate degree of corporatism, possibilities of democracy, both socialism and liberalism in moderation, and no definite trend towards strong corporatism. The snap-shot is inconclusive and composed of fragments, for I have no single method for analysing society. It suggests a political forecast rather akin to the meteorological forecast that covers most possible weathers. In fact I find myself provisionally poised on a point of uncertainty and non-decision about corporatism. I also find in my snap-shot of Britain as it now is a quasi-elitist system. There is certainly a radical inequality of power, yet elite power is significantly distributed and divided — how far is controversial, but it seems to me less well coordinated than in several other industrial countries, than is suggested by Marxists, or than is evident in earlier ages when Britain elites were allegedly less effete. At one and the same time state power over some groups has increased and yet the degeneration of the former liberal consensus round Butskellism and the scramble for power among interests groups, as well as the diffusion of power downwards to shop, office and factory floors could be seen as an expansion of democracy. There are types of group conflict that you would not expect to be manifested in a strong corporate state. The corporatism, such as it is, is moderate, and at most it might be in transition towards something stronger. Indeed it may be argued that it is the very weakness of state corporatism which is a main element in the present ills of Britain. Thus the segmentation of society into many groups, some of them small but with coercive power, and the competitive scramble to which high costs are attached for most or all, is not a symptom of the birth of organic unity found in a strong corporate state, but of a crisis in a liberal democracy. As Samuel Brittan sees it, the right to pursue self-interest has been carried too far; or as R.M. Unger puts it (*Law in Modern Society*, Glencoe: Free Press, 1975), there is an intense need in liberal society for organised power existing alongside a baffling inability to justify any kind of power at all.

Going further with this line of reasoning, there appears

to be a loosening of the disciplines and restraints on which liberal, industrial societies have depended. It is arguable that this is an important underlying cause, not merely an effect, of the present and recently high rates of inflation. It has been argued that the inflationary spiral threatens to fling us into an accelerating and self-defeating process of breakdown. The frustrations which exacerbate inter-group conflict are increased with each disruption of the economy, and the increasing economic scramble may produce greater disruptions. If this thesis were accepted, then, apart from historical predictions, there might be strong temptations to prescribe strong corporatism as an antidote to breakdown: perhaps it might capped by a council recruited from industry and supported by centrists in all parties, as suggested by Lords Robens and Beeching. Such advocacy obliges us to ask what costs and benefits, economic and moral, would fall to us all, or to groups such as producers, voluntary associations, universities and schools, welfare-service clients, and so on, if strong corporatism were instituted. However, so obscure is the future that one might just as readily predict that strong corporatism will develop in a linear fashion from existing trends as that it will erupt after an experience of radical run-down or breakdown due, not to an excess of corporatism, but to an insufficiency of it.

Be that as it may, I shall now elaborate on my reasons for portraying Britain as only moderately a corporate state.

First, there are highly organised, independently powerful interest groups operating in a competitive context. Interest group activity confirms not the all-embracing ideology of unity and higher purpose required by a strong corporate state, but is an extension to groups and organisations of liberal individualist ideology. Much conflict is limited; objectives and methods are typically within bounds. The dominant belief system makes conflict legitimate. Whatever may be our humanist or Christian, socialist or aesthetic distaste for self-seeking behaviours in an acquisitive society, that is the dominant mode of behaviour in the interest-group system.

It might be thought, however, that this system is being undermined by a decline in law and order; many instances will be cited, including some unions' refusal to co-operate with the Heath government's Industrial Relations Act, 1972. Conventions of self-restraint may well be weakening. But many occasions in the previous history of liberal democracy have prompted citizens, some in small groups, to thwart the law through non-cooperation. Not every resistance is justified or promotes liberty, but the power to limit what government may do is not the kind of power one would expect in an effectively organised corporate state.

Rightly or wrongly, then, legitimacy is conferred on group tactics of self-protection and self-aggrandisement. In the bargaining process groups justify to themselves short-run sacrifices by weighing their long-run self interest, not by subordination to overriding common objectives. What is lacking are agreed criteria for the just distribution of sacrifices and rewards, but not justifications for refusing to make sacrifices. Recalcitrant groups may excite adverse public opinion, but are not usually suppressed, even though, as many directors and managers well know, the balance of advantages has been changing unfavourably from their point of view. Further more, the adjustment of claims among organised groups is pragmatic and instrumental. Most groups take *ad hoc* decisions on trade-offs and adopt *ad hoc* ways of assessing the utilities of collective action when they respond to appeals, threats or crises. For example, the TUC's agreement on wage restraint has been conditioned by calculations about the impact of wage-pushed inflation on unemployment. More generally, their co-operation on incomes policy has required a package covering productivity, prices, all incomes, taxation and social security (D.K. Stout, 'Incomes Policy' in S.E. Finer, ed., *Adversary Politics and Electoral Reform*, London: Wigram, 1975).

There is still vigorous competition, though with limits set

by prevailing ideas of justice and by an unequal distribution of power within corporate society, for wealth, incomes, status and power. Scrambles for wages and salaries are usually settled by negotiation and compromise; there are shifting alliances; and haggling is backed by overt attempts to bid for support within a group or outside, but with no assurance of getting it because of the independence of factions and groups. Politics still involves much log-rolling. Many refusals to co-operate are not punished directly; and periodic tidal waves towards confrontation are usually broken by a series of small bargains, not by the power of a nearly omnipotent government. Politics is refractory, not unified. Some groups abuse their advantages, resort to direct action, and more groups are expressing their grievances aggressively while still others are getting into the game. Of course most significant competitors are large and powerful; but power is also held by small, technologically or administratively critical, groups. There is much inequality of power, with many interests unorganised or readily sacrificed.

It is only against this background that one can grasp the claim, made by Samuel Brittan, that public goods, such as raising productivity or reducing the rate of inflation, lose out in the contest among self-seeking sectional interests. If we do not have the pre-Tudor problem of holding feudal barons in check, we at least have the problem of competitive interest groups gaining advantages at the expense of the public interest or the liberty of others. That is always the risk inherent in a liberal polity; the bonds of self-restraint may become tenuous or fragile. But to phrase the issues in these terms is to underline one's scepticism about the application of the strong version of state corporatism to the present situation and perhaps to any foreseeable future situation. It suggests instead a possible surfiet of liberty, not its counterfeit — a self-defeating liberty, not liberty's absence — a liberty advantaging sharks, not timid minnows.

Contrary to what would be expected in a full-blooded corporate state which firmly stipulates an economic strategy, there has been and still is little agreement on economic and industrial strategy in Britain. True, for some years after 1945 there seemed to be much agreement on major economic objectives (on growth, low inflation, high employment and balanced payments) and on many methods. But in recent years there has been less consensus, certainly on the relative priority of these objectives; for example, the latitutude opened up on the pursuit of full employment may be carried still further by the influence of monetarism. There is very weak consensus on fiscal and monetary policy, as witnessed by discord over public expenditure restrictions; on the level and type of government intervention (e.g. the National Enterprise Board); and on the fundamental causes of our economic maladies. There is at best conditional and highly qualified agreement on the machinery of economic management and strategy development. So even major institutional arrangements are in question. There are also repeated calls for a bipartisan approach to economic policy; such calls are met with scepticism, and actual overtures across the party divide are usually spurned by the potential partner. Indeed calls for coalition government rest on the untested assumption that the vast majority would prefer it in practice.

There is no overall national plan for the next five or ten years. Long-run planning, indicative rather than directive, seems unrealistic in the UK context of divided opinion and power. NEDO, though surviving changes of government, still operates through *ad hoc* adaptation to a series of running crises, providing a medium to keep people talking when the division of power makes concerted action unlikely. There are no realistic overall targets, and no general parameters of economic development set by a relatively politically independent group of government strategists. The current work on sectors of industry in

NEDO is a modest attempt to deal piece-meal with relatively detailed, short-run, practically remediable problems, with so far no overall strategy of government support for export-leading industries. Indeed there is little prospect of real agreement on common objectives, and log-rolling may be involved in the hard decisions on which sectors and firms will receive high priority.

As the machinery is rather fluid and the policies vague, businesses' uncertainties are aggravated. Although there is now much uncertainty in business round the world, the contrast between Britain on the one hand and, on the other, the histories of Sweden, Japan and Germany — and until quite recently, France — is striking. Britain cannot match their records of sustained co-operation and target-setting; their social solidarity and discipline as well as their government machinery make them more appropriate for the label 'corporate state'. Of course I exaggerate to make the point. It is not that Sweden, for example, is a powerful corporate state, yet her economic performance has been excellent. In fact the impact that organised groups have there is enormous; they add up to an extra-constitutional power system to the extent that parties and the legislature, as is often suggested about the UK, merely confer political legitimacy on decisions whose outlines are settled elsewhere.

Nevertheless the plain point is that economic and industrial policies in the UK are open to politicking on a large scale, not to direction from above. It is very difficult, as we have seen for many years, for 'non-partisan' agencies such as NIC, NBPI, and PIB in the pay field, or even NEDO, to achieve stable positions of plausible non-partisanship and to develop authority: not because they intend to be partisan or their personnel are defective, but because they are crushed by the determined partisanship of the contending groups over which they are supposed to ride herd. One index of how hard Britain is to govern is that when new responsibilities for control and co-ordination over the economy are imposed on a new agency, its powers are grossly unequal to those possessed by others.

Furthermore, interest groups insistently claim to intrude upon established processes of consultation or to challenge the implementation of policies. As the balances of power change among the trade-unions as well as within each of them, that is reflected in what can be said or done by the TUC's leaders. The vast and cumbersome consultative network may still be breached; newly activated pressure groups, like the British Institute of Management, seek a place in the higher councils.

There are a few fixed policies and purposes. There is often muddle, ad hocery raised to the level of principle, and frequent change to meet short-run contingencies and pressures. Government policy is vulnerable, operates with scant room for manoeuvre, and often has to be inconsistent. The periodic adoption and abandonment of incomes policy may have produced a cumulatively higher rate of inflation than would have been the case had there been consistently a policy or none at all. That, like the position of the IRC in the past and speculation about the continued existence of NEB in future should the government change hands (or about the future of incomes policy or NEDO), highlights the kind of government by U-turn to which we have been subject. We get radical changes with each new party in office, and changes of equal or greater magnitude while a party is in office. We get two governments for the price of every election.

In saying this I have no wish to score a cheap point against politicians nor to reinforce British convictions that they are now among the worst governed people in the world. I wish to refer to the fundamentals of the political power distribution. There are not strong corporatist tendencies to merge organisational power at the top and produce long-run policies. Rather there is in Britain, in addition to the normal uncertainties of the economic

market, a notable degree of uncertainty stemming from the
political-administrative market. The latter market has its
own changing balances of power; the kinds of change it
produces in government policy is a symptom of
government's sensitivity to the power of groups. Of course,
the 'political market' is powerfully shaped by the
organisations of capital and labour, but that concept does
help, I think, to explain the British style of government:
change through periodic elections and government by *volte-
face* in between elections.

This point is supported by reference not merely to the
past fifteen years, but to the present position of the
Opposition. The Conservative Party appears to have no
settled position over time. In the 30s, 40s and early 50s it
looked more corporatist about government-industry
partnership that it now does (Nigel Harris, *Competition and the
Corporate Society*, London: Methuen, 1972). It therefore seems
to be heading towards policies that would, if it were to take
office, negate or reverse many present policies and probably
intensify conflict over economic strategy. That prospect
hardly suggests the stuff of strong corporatism.

I had noted much earlier that one appeal of the corporate
state concept is that it blurs the distinction between public
and private in the economy. The government's role in
stabilising an ailing system, its reciprocal action and
reaction with the major economic organisations, and even
the interlocking or exchange of personnel, produce the
blur. But a closer look at the realities should warn us against
too quickly superceding the orthodox distinction implied by
the concept of a mixed economy. For in reality within the
constraints each imposes on the other the agents and
organisations still have scope for choice; indeed choices are
still made by businesses and their suppliers, by investors and
financiers and consumers — all in the private sector on the
one hand — and by government and its ancillary
production organisations on the other hand. There are two

distinguishable systems of resource allocation; they interact strongly but are not merged. In other words, there is a market sector, albeit highly imperfect competitively and much interfered with and influenced by government, and a public sector in which resource allocation is through a political system and its central phenomena are taxation and public expenditure. Integration of the two allocation systems is piecemeal, and there is gross uncertainty as to how the two systems jointly maximise and distribute welfare. A strong corporate state would, I think, develop an integrated strategy concerning the best use of resources in both sectors. But the UK shows virtually no sign of such development, even though ideas about it are implicit in much ideological controversy, e.g. standards of just distribution which attempt comprehensive estimates of both private and public goods.

In any case, what is this *state* that manages a mixed economy or, more strongly, directs a coherent economic strategy? Not only does it do many different things involving many layers in diverse agencies which are related co-operatively and combatively, it is also replete with counterveiling powers large and small. Government may be the greatest power, but internally its powers are divided and often ill-coordinated. It is an enormous machine with an internally elaborate division of labour; it has severe management problems; and in spite of the Cabinet system, horizontal integration at the top is relatively weak, especially when ministers have their own followings and senior civil servants their own clientele. Whitehall vibrates to the sound of grinding axes. Each political leadership is itself an uneasy coalition; yet offsetting the prominence enjoyed by top politicians is the undoubted influence of civil servants — not the service seen as a cohesive body, but as diversely constituted teams and tribes. In spite of a history of Treasury control and the development of inter-departmental committees, much lateral integration remains an aim rather than an achievement. Moreover, much in the education, training and tradition of senior civil servants renders them unlikely to run a strong corporate state along the lines of 'Great Britain Limited'.

If one adds to this picture the one drawn earlier of the interest-group system, it would not be difficult to conceive how government is not yet master of the powers it seeks to constrain. Its own unwieldy and internally divided nature, coupled with the freedom of its potential partners or subordinates, places it not above the conflict but suggests that it or each of its parts is another party to the conflict. Government is imbedded within the pressure-group system as a whole; it is itself a sub-system of the whole.

Instead of setting clearly defined goals and regulations, as would occur in a strong corporate state, the operations of government look more like feverish attempts to square circles, and to patch together elaborate trade-offs in which different groups inside and outside government make different trade-off assessments over different time-scales. Government cannot impose its will except on the weak; when a group is weak or lacks determination or a prudent regard for its own interests, government can have its way regulating and prescribing. But we have repeatedly seen how governments cannot compel investments and savings (though it can, contrary to its wishes, inhibit either), cannot except within severe constraints control the balance of payments or the exchange value of sterling, and cannot hold in check many of its clientele groups — nor it seems the sectional interests of civil servants themselves. As one writer has put it, British government looks like the Sorcerer's Apprentice (A. King, *Why is Britain Becoming Harder to Govern?*, London: BBC, 1976, ch. 1).

If there is failure to achieve or even plausibly to formulate economic objectives, it is not for want of constitutional authority, but because of the costs and constraints generated by an internally divided parliamentary and administrative system which is both cause and effect of a highly divided economy and society. The difficulties which governments have in making an impact are well illustrated by the fact that, in the fight against inflation, the price of TUC co-operation on wage restraint has been price and dividend controls. Such controls are thought (though not unqualifiedly) to inhibit investment. But if that contributes to higher unemployment, how can union support be enlisted for anti-inflationary cuts in public expenditure which would also contribute to unemployment? Within such a closed circle of political pressure and economic constraint it is virtually inevitable that government should be groping — and that while it continues to grope more radical palliatives should be advocated, which further polarise positions. For instance, on one side it is asked whether the constraint on cutting inflationary public expenditure should not be weakened by reducing trade-union power. And on the other side it is reasoned that, if price controls are required for union co-operation and yet reinforce disincentives to invest arising from hyper-inflation and high interest rates, then should not government take more powers to acquire or control investment? In an economic context where the private enterprise is highly dependent on retained profits as a source of investment, the kind of polarisation just outlined can have nothing less than life or death consequences for the enterprise.

Although crudely formulated, the question about government control over investments invites the inquiry whether such a step would represent a doctrinaire move towards socialism or, as it may seem in some other countries in the advanced industrial world, a pragmatic response by government to unavoidable pressures arising from the economic system. Indeed in other places the government's role in investment is seen as a vitally dynamic element in a healthy, growing economy. But in Britain the circumscribing circle of pressure and constraint, based on self-interest and ideology, suggests that we are not analysing a strong corporate state but a case of nearly 'enfeebled government' (Andrew Shonfield, *The Listener*, 18 March 1976). In Britain government actions in the name of economic necessity are often seen by others as socialist; or actions which it names socialist are often ones which it must probably take anyway for the sake of economic survival, given the acceptance of existing political rights. That this does often happen is one measure of the kind of confusion and polarisation from which government action springs and to which it also contributes.

For many businessmen I suppose this analysis will seem one-sided. For them government increasingly means a big stick or clumsy attempts to help; the litany of recent legislation is enough to bear out the point. Yet if Richard Crossman's diaries have any credibiltiy, they convey a sense of despair about government's immobility — its incapacity to take major, long-run decisions year in and year out on sterling, inflation, union-power, and devolution. Even the settlement of one great issue, membership of the EEC, had to be put out to referendum. Crossman's picture of splits in Cabinets, departments and parties, even if overdrawn, suggests wide scope for petty power struggles and expediential compromises, not the clear-sighted and firm pursuit of national economic goals (supposing these could be conceived in terms commanding very wide agreement across the political spectrum).

From this account it is possible to conclude that what the UK needs is stronger government which brushes aside the pettiness of intra-party feuds, the doctrinaire rigidities of party ideologues which irresponsibly widen the terms of inter-party competition, and the selfishness of interest groups. But that is to imply that what we have not got is a potent corporate state: it is to indicate some of the forces which stand in the way of its creation. Yet many of these forces are within the fabric of British liberalism and democracy. It may be that widespread disillusionment with the present system's economic performance will eventually produce a lurch towards strong corporatism, but on this possibility my crystal ball is cloudy.

Having mentioned the political system and the alleged vices of 'adversary politics' in the party arena, another dimension of the distribution of power must be explored briefly. Having suggested that horizontal integration among top groups within government and between it and the elites of the major interest groups is relatively weak in terms of what a strong corporate state would look like. I shall now suggest that vertical integration within many organisations is both weaker than would be required in a strong corporate state and one cause of the difficulty in achieving close horizontal integration at the top of society.

Whatever may be thought about the irrelevance of the party system to Britain's economic problems, or the damage U-turns and ideological frivolities have caused, there is persistent evidence that party leaderships have considerable difficulties in managing their followers inside and outside Parliament. In recent years more powers have developed at the base, if not the actual grass-roots, of the parties, as evidenced by conflicts inside constituencies over the re-nomination of sitting MPs.

More generally, many interest groups are highly decentralised as organisations, allowing activist factions to make the running. Elitism in such organisations must be seen as significantly qualified. Leaders in professions such as engineering, medicine and teaching find it difficult to control their rank and file or to prevent schism. Negotiating positions of elites may therefore be limited by activists operating in the lower ranks; integration between the peaks of associations may then be weakened.

Unions are often repositories of power struggles among factions. Bargaining in industry, which once looked as if it

might become effectively national, thereby lending weight
to a corporate-state thesis, has moved in recent decades
towards the plant and shop-floor. Even industry-wide
agreements are now considered remarkable, but in any case
subject to wide local variations. Notwithstanding apathy
and opportunities for manipulation, it is possible that a
kind of micro-democracy has advanced in the trade-union
movement and is now more widespread than in any other
advanced industrial society. Such devolution of power to
thousands of small working units and shop-stewards can
make the leaders of the TUC appear like the generals of a
phantom army. Given this decentralisation of power, there
must be much negotiation and compromise within the
union movement; and at the highest levels of tri-partite
negotiations, the ability of the TUC to 'deliver up' the
workers must be severely limited. Agreements at the
corporate-state level are therefore precariously dependent
on co-operation from below. Hence the tension and drama
surrounding any attempt by a small group to breach such
agreements. The crudity of recent wage-control recipes so
far used in Britain, even if seen as a valuable check on wage-
drift, reveals the incapacity of leaders of big battalions and
government to develop mechanisms of a strong corporate
state capable of holding small groups and individuals in
line. Though most attention naturally focusses on weak
vertical integration within unions and the TUC as a whole,
the very loose-knit structure of the CBI and most
employers' federations also fits into this picture.

In further support of this thesis one might add that the
introduction of legally prescribed forms of workers'
participation in management, though likely to make
further inroads on management prerogatives, may do little
to improve vertical integration of employee and employer
associations. If anything, such schemes may solidify at
company or plant level powers already devolved
downwards within unions, and thus strengthen the many

bases of power that could operate against programmes sponsored by corporate-state elites. Furthermore, unions that favour participation schemes tend to see them as extensions of collective bargaining, and as, therefore, the acquisition of further levers of control over the policy of an enterprise. Far from adopting the ethos of close co-operation and solidarity characteristic of corporatism, many unions welcome worker-directors as a means of gaining power in an adversary relationship with employers. No doubt the hope will be held out to directors and managers of the eventual development of attitudes of non-antagonism or corporative partnership; but their own present mistrust of such rhetoric is likely to be justified.

Lying equally in the foreground of public consciousness today is another fissure in British society; the movement towards devolution of power to Scotland and Wales. The arguments, high-minded and low, for devolution are too complex to rehearse here; and the historical causes are multiple. But the movement, now sanctioned by a government seeking conciliation of powers it perceives to be beyond its control, is another indication of a trend towards decentralisation and lack of trust in the central political powers in party and state administration. Whether one takes devolution to be a sign of healthy democracy or pathological breakdown, one fact stands out a mile: it is hardly evidence for the present existence of strong state corporatism or for a linear trend towards it.

Devolution will amount to a process of elaborating a kind of social contract within Great Britain. In fact, underlying much of my scepticism about strong state corporatism and my inclination towards a pluralistic, quasi-elitist, quasi-democratic version of the corporate state, is one further reflection about the British term 'the social contract', coined to cover tripartite agreements reached by government, TUC and CBI. The very term implies the existence of a still partially liberal, though corporate, society. The bargaining, threats of non-cooperation, public attacks, the reciprocal setting of constraints, the internal divisions of each contracting group, and uncertainty over whether any 'contract', even if adhered to for one year, will be renewed after re-negotiation, provide telling evidence of the incomplete character of British state corporatism. The voluntary, competitive nature of 'the social contract', together with its highly uncertain means of enforcing performance, need not be laboured.

All the evidence I have so far cited leads me to one risky piece of general speculation with which to end. Whatever may be said about the costs, public and private, of Britain's economic malaise, the culture does not appear to display strongly what may be called the values of solidarity. It is as if the values of political liberalism and economic competition, developed in the eighteenth and nineteenth centuries, are still bearing fruit in the attitudes and actions of the whole culture. Everyone points backwards to the experience of solidarity during the Second World War, when danger and hardship were shared experiences, and endurance and tolerant good-cheer were shared virtues. However I suspect, again risking broad generalisation, that for reasons difficult to fathom, a sense of conformity to higher national purpose and social solidarity may be stronger in Japan or Germany or Sweden. Britain is not only dominated by the instrumental, competitive approach to group interaction; it has long depended on a spirit of mutual accommodation, toleration and incremental change ('muddling through'). The Japanese sociologist, Chie Nakane, has remarked on the deep integration of the typical Japanese person in his organisations, especially at the work-place, and on the manner in which personal autonomy is traded off against security and emotional support from the group (*The Times*, 2 Sept. 1970). But it is unclear how such micro-solidarity contributes to national solidarity — is it by weakening the competitive potentialities of critical associations such as trade-unions? Be that as it may, many other commentators have remarked on the high degree of collaboration there is within the Japanese elites of government and industry, though again this does not appear to include trade-union leaders. Undoubtedly every analysis of national character and institutional arrangements reaches for an over-simplifying general answer to account for national differences.

Nevertheless, in abandoning the normal circumspection of my profession, I would emphasise about Britain the relative weakness of a common acceptance of 'primary virtues' (Alastair MacIntyre, *Secularization and Moral Change*, London: Oxford University Press, 1967, Chapter 2). This is not to say there are no common moral denominators: the question is what they consist in and why they are accepted. Britain is culturally and morally a remarkably diverse society. The aims of collective action and the boundaries of behaviour are set either by each group in terms not accepted by other groups or by a coincidence of self-interested groups. The codes of different groups are significantly different, in spite of overlaps and mutual absorption. Historically trade-unionism stands for solidarity within the work-group and neighbourhood; the middle-classes historically stand for individualism and its associated virtues of self-reliance and ambition; and historic assumptions about leadership in the ruling classes and public schools stand at a polar extreme in relation to the traditional ethos of trade-unionism. Although much of all this is thought to belong only to the past, the residues strongly persist. Furthermore, the bulk of society for more than a century has not been practising Christian; and the fusion of Christianity with upper class and Establishment institutions and their codes of natural superiority and responsibility may have increased social divisions. Finer-textured distinctions persist as well. For reasons imbedded in our cultural and educational inheritance, there are, compared with other nations, remarkable distinctions made between pure and applied scientists, between scientists and technologists, between the arts and the sciences, and between ˚thinkers and doers. Sharp organisational boundaries exist between business, the civil service and the universities; personal contacts and exchanges of personnel are infrequent, and the mutual incomprehension and suspicion which exist suggest, not a highly integrated and coherently linked cluster of elites, but remarkable gulfs among them.

There are, in short, important yet puzzling sub-cultural divisions. Social class is only one type of such division. The most vaunted homogeneity of Britain — the most urban of urban nations, a national press, truly national parties, an established church — is only one side of a complex society.

If this analysis is valid, then it is more necessary for the body politic to be held together by recourse to 'secondary virtues' — that is, not the objectives and principles that mean most to any particular group or which sharply distinguish one group from another, but the values which provide a *modus vivendi* for all groups. It may be this need for peaceful co-existence among culturally different and antagonistic groups which explains the peculiar importance for so long in British public life of such secondary virtues as fair play, abiding by the rules of the game, not rocking the boat, making negotiable demands, and tolerating but not understanding alien values. The alternative to this is the imposition of one group's primary values and substantive goals or ideals upon the whole society, the last attempt at which, in the seventeenth century, brought about civil war.

A society constituted in the way described is bound to feel that it has no overriding and unifying *raison d'être*, or to wonder what values underpin its structure, for example, what fair play is *for*. At times its very basis in the secondary virtues of liberalism may seem precarious in the face of militancy or fanaticism. Yet when the virtues of moderation are appealed to against extremism, the radical theorist is then tempted to stigmatise moderation and the whole range of secondary virtues as part of the ideology of the dominant class.

Of course this whole line of speculation is a gross simplification; but it has been adopted for the sake of making vivid the general thesis that much in the value-system of Britain is inimical to the establishment of a powerful corporate state. However, for reasons stated earlier, I can make no confident prediction about the future; in particular, one cannot rule out a strong corporate state evolving from deep revulsion against the adversary politics of parties and interest groups. Indeed political systems, like economic systems, can change radically and yet be at odds with the intentions and values of most people. Hence my preference for uncertainty over certainty.

IV

The foregoing comments on trends towards or away from a strong corporate state in Britain have, I think, major implications for our understanding of the business enterprise. How we are to understand its objectives, methods, form of internal government and politics, its social responsibilities, its relations to its external environment, and what it can or cannot do as an initiator and manager of social action depends largely upon what we can expect from an analysis of the political context. And what is extracted will obviously affect our conception of what types of people, with what goals and skills, will be needed in managing the enterprise of the foreseeable future. Unfortunately my exploration of these issues must now be deferred to another occasion.